MAN
EVOLVING

Confessions
about monogamy,
passion and
broken hearts.

BERNARDO MOYA

A Man Evolving
© 2022 by Bernardo Moya

ISBN: 978-1-64810-181-6

Published by Perfect Publishing Co.

Printed in the United States of America

DEDICATION

This book is dedicated to...

To my mum and the unconditional love, she gave me,
for trusting me and allowing me to believe I was able
and capable of doing anything I put my head to.
I miss you terribly although I know you are still with
me every step of the way.

ACKNOWLEDGMENTS

Christopher Keith and Alicia Wilcox for their editing expertise, tips and advice.

Susan Crossman for her valuable feedback and guidance on the final edit.

To Catalina Federosky and Gervasio Troche for the beautiful illustrations.

And all the editing expertise from Sally Brown, Jack Black and Billy Blue.

To Ken Ronchon for supporting me, believing in me and being so motivated in publishing this book.

TABLE OF CONTENTS

DISCLAIMER

A Man Evolving. I am a man who has made many mistakes and continues to make them. But as a man, I should honour, acknowledge, and share what I feel and not keep my emotions bottled up, as many men do. Male suicide is one of the biggest killers of men, depression is at an all-time high. I have been lucky enough to be operational myself, as during quite a few stages of my life I feel I have been a non-diagnosed semi-depressed man. I never had therapy and I never sought help for many of the encounters life has thrown at me. So *A Man Evolving* is my way of opening up and saying many of the things I should have said and done many years ago.

I am human, but as a man, they way I love has evolved. I also have a responsibility to become better, a better man, a better human, a better person. Men in general do, just like Uncle Ben said (if you'll remember he's the uncle of Spiderman/Peter Parker), *"with great power comes great responsibility"* and as self-help author Mark Manson said, with *"great responsibility comes great power."*

A Man Evolving began with the idea of a "comprehensive" book that intended to unravel and present what love is, because "love is not what you or think it is."

What do I mean by that? I'll explain in the next section.

This book began as a journey to elevate my consciousness and expose myself to a higher level of vulnerability. By sharing my findings, I hope that you, too, will be able to elevate your own consciousness and come to more inspiring conclusions, as well.

I appreciate life, and also understand we are mortals who know not when our time will end. Like you, I have lost a few friends and loved ones. For me, this has happened recently. I also have some close friends and family experiencing serious health issues.

Lumped together with ageing, falling out of love, and breaking hearts, my position as a global events promoter and author (with a little wisdom thrown in for good measure), has opened my eyes to the words unsaid throughout our lives, to the way we prioritise the wrong things, to how we become so materialistic, and to the sad fact that we accumulate goods, "things," instead of memories, positive experiences, and emotions.

Although everyone has an ego to some extent, I've learnt how to put mine to the side. I also keep it well hidden, but I am smart enough to know I have done some great things in my life, some of which have contributed to encouraging growth and learning in the personal development world. I have also witnessed the fact that several people in the "self-improvement" business are missing the mark. Love has to play a bigger role in everyday conversation! We also have to be kinder and elevate our consciousness in the process.

Let me say it's been very difficult to write this book. It's the only time I have felt comfortable sharing my innermost thoughts, my deepest feelings. I have had to experience what I made others experience. After all, this is a crucial part of elevating one's consciousness.

I have shared the content with my former wife, lovers, loved ones, and close friends. Whether they chose to read it was up to them. I have not written this book to hurt anyone or level scores; I am simply trying to be open with my thoughts, experiences, vulnerability, flaws, and mistakes.

I am no expert on the complex topic of Love. I am NOT a therapist or certified coach. I don't consider myself a writer (although I write). I am definitely not a poet! I am a man sharing his thoughts, feelings, and experiences in and out of love. I have done a fair amount of work in NLP (Neuro-Linguistic Programming); I have done a fair amount of work in NLP (Neuro-Linguistic Programming), and have worked and promoted the co-creator for NLP for over a decade. I have read vast selection books, and it has all brought me to a point in my life where I am questioning what love is or possibly is not.

Not everyone is romantic or feels compelled to express their feelings. Still, humans need and desire true love. Don't we? Trust me, when you're on your deathbed and heaven beckons, you won't be thinking about your shoes, cars, or record collections. They're not coming with you.

So here is my disclaimer: I am simply a man, en evolving man, an older heterosexual man, with old, engrained views on what love is supposed to mean. I grew up in an era when women were still finding their way to what was then called "liberation" and a bewildered generation of men reluctantly, and with great hesitation, "allowed" them to play a bigger role in the world, even while still getting in their way and, at times, trying to outright stop them from succeeding; some of us even felt comfortable in the idea that we should decide what women should be entitled to do.

Many of us are still doing that. Meanwhile, Western views on sexuality have shifted seismically over the years,, and the "rules" have been changing continuously. Much as I have sought to keep up, I am still a product of my upbringing, my times, and my own limitations. While I have consistently tried not to "limit" my thinking in all things, I wear the blinders that my values, beliefs, personality and character impose upon me. I see myself as a work in progress , a flawed man who dreams of becoming con- sistently expansive, that I put this book before you.

So, within this disclaimer, I want to clearly state I accept all genders and sexual inclinations and none of my comments are intended to offend anyone; that being said, I am privileged to enjoy the right to express my thoughts and feelings freely and ask that this book be a "judgement free zone." Haven't we judged, and been judged, enough already? Let's set all that aside and open to vulnerable conversation and the humility of exploration.

There is some rawness here, and some of the statements I make may strike a discordant note with some people. I strongly believe that honesty is key, and you will only hear from my authentic self...so, much as I ask for your patience and com- passion in this effort to share my thoughts on the experience of Love, I also request you to withhold any judgement you may be inclined to pass. Open your heart to the possibility of "something more" here that will answer a question you are seeking to resolve. Open your heart to the possibility of growing. And just plain open your heart.

In this book, I aim to be empathetic towards everyone on the human spectrum, regardless of nationality, gender, or sexual orientation. We are, after all, one race. So, any comments that appear to exclude anyone are a result of my own inability to express inclusion effectively, rather than any intention on my part to knowingly exclude someone.

Above all, I do hope we can agree that any form of love is great and beautiful.

You see, as I mentioned, we live in a world of judgment. Everyone is guilty of judging someone without context. It's human nature, exacerbated by the advent of the Internet, which puts everyone and anyone in the spotlight and exposes them to criticism.

Some may judge me when I say I have failed as a man, in so many ways I would need hours to compile a list.

I failed as a husband, and I let my former wife down.

I was a cheater. I cheated on my wife towards the end of my marriage, even at the end, with a friend. There is no excuse for the pain I caused; no justification.

We met at age 15, became a couple at 19, and once kids came into the equation, that was it for me. Even though we were very young and naïve, I was brought up with the understanding that you marry, stay loyal to your partner, and stay together forever.

Cheating is unacceptable and unjustifiable. Once you discover you are not happy (which was not necessarily my case, because I loved my family and my wife) you should move on. Maybe in hindsight, I should have discussed it with her and separated sooner, maybe we should have left each other ten years sooner.

I want to point out here before I continue, that I loved and adored my ex-wife, she was a phenomenal lover and partner. Wicked sense of humour, beautiful, sexy, with a very big heart; she had spent years supporting me and bringing up our beautiful family. I felt I was taken for granted but to a degree, I took her for granted too. But I always have appreciated her deep love and commitment to me and our relationship. She's a very special and classy lady and always has been. All I have is a deep love for her and gratitude. With her sense of humour, she would probably have said suggested I title the book: *Simply a very very stupid man!*

Break-ups with young ones are common nowadays, and unless the relationship is toxic, I don't think it's the best option for kids and their development. Divorce certainly wasn't the best option at the time, and perhaps this was selfish of me. As a result, I remained in an unhappy marriage for a long time as my wife and I had drifted apart.

My biggest failure was as a father. I should have been a better father. I was too focused on making money and lost many valuable years with my kids; I should have communicated how much they meant to me more, harming the relationship we once had. I'm sure I'm not the only man who messed up and regretted it. And learning to forgive ourselves takes time.

My lover and I found solace in each other at a time when we were both hurting. I regret how it happened, but with her, there were no regrets. She, my lover, was what I needed and helped me navigate a challenging time. Our fling lasted briefly and then became a committed relationship for four years, and her love and support meant everything to me.

The thing is, my actions hurt a lot of people, people I loved the most, and nowadays I feel to a degree like an outsider looking into my life, into my family. I feel a disconnect from my kids which I hope I can eventually make right. In the end, I did what I thought was best. I can't take back what I did, but I can now look at myself in the mirror again. I didn't want to continue to be part of the big lie, which is what I think happens in many other marriages too.

The world has changed dramatically from the last generation to this one. Long-term marriages, monogamy, and imposed structures based on our culture and religion are changing before our eyes, and many "norms" have been relegated to the past. I highly recommend you read *Sex at Dawn* by Christopher Ryan and Cacilda Letha. It's a great read and really breaks down the reality around monogamy.

Look, I am being honest here.
Have you judged me already?
Have you?
I mean, have you ever cheated? If so, how often?
Are you cheating?
Have you ever fancied or fantasised about other people?
Most importantly...
Are you living a lie?

If that isn't your case, good for you.

I have been judged and condemned by "close friends" who no longer wish to stay connected with me. Despite years and years of friendship and amazing memories—most of these were in my house and involved me paying, and cooking and everyone seemed to enjoy themselves very much; they enjoyed me and my company at the time, but that all changed.

But it hurt that none of them ever tried to understand why I gave up on thirty years of marriage and moved on. No one started a single conversation with me on the topic. I felt ostracized and judged – had none of those people ever put a foot wrong in their live?

Know what? I'll take my chances with God.

Culture is changing, has changed...but is it changing quickly enough?

I mean, nowadays, if we meet someone who thinks differently than we do, has a different stance on politics or religion or is not the same skin colour or sexual orientation as us, we seem to "cancel" or criticise easily.

Many people can be emotionally unintelligent or lack empathy or understanding when they disagree with an action or statement.

I was a typical old-school male! Relationships and partnerships are very different nowadays.

The reason I decided to change my ways was because most of my friends seemed to operate with the same kind of mindset I had, and I wasn't happy continuing to be that way.

When publishing my previous book, The *Question: Find Your True Purpose*, which is packed with questions and honest discussions, I asked readers some tough questions and I choose not to ask them of myself. But to become a better man, a congruent man, it was necessary for me to do so.

So, the book to a degree forced me to take action, to make a decision, to be honest with myself, my wife, and my family. I wasn't happy in so many ways. I needed to do something about it.

The type of questions I was ignoring were like these ones:

Are You Happy?
What's stopping you from being happy?
Is something or someone holding you back?
Are you honest with yourself?
Are you honest with your loved ones?

What do you need to do?
When?
What happens if you don't?

So that's where I am now. Sharing my focus on learning from my mistakes, questioning and addressing thoughts around love and relationships.

But I'd like to state clearly that I am a romantic and I believe in true and honest love, and I'd like to have a long-term partner in a near future.

What I ask from you is this:

For you to give me a chance to explain why I think traditional marriage is questionable or might have an expiry date. And by that, I mean if we do marry, (and it might not be necessary anymore), do we have to marry forever?

Does it have to be forever?

Can it be forever?

Is it reasonable to expect that anymore?

By expecting it to be forever do we put too much pressure on that relationship?

And if we do, can we be monogamous?

What I hope with this book is to help create and set expectations.

I know many people do believe in the long term and forever. I would hope that when I am blessed to have another partner one day (if I finally have one) that we can be there for each other and enjoy every day, living in the now.

I just think we need to be realistic with our expectations and enjoy love when we find it. Embrace it and cherish it and the only way to keep it alive if there is a true and honest communication with our needs and desires, whatever your sexual inclination or gender.

The truth is, the world is changing quickly.

The intention of this book is:

For men and women to feel the same degree and integrity of love and quality of love that I have experienced with my partners.
For men, in particular, to be more honest and open with their feelings.
For couples to communicate more and express how they feel.
For men to stop thinking with their dicks all the time.
For women to stop living a lie or accepting a dishonest situation.

SPECIAL THANK YOU TO:

I say, "thank you" to my ex-wife for giving me so many beautiful memories, amazing kids, commitment, love, and adoration. I send my dearest apologies for the pain I have caused you. Thank you for being such a wonderful mum to our kids and being such a classy lady all your life. I love you, and always will.

To my daughter who I hurt and disappointed so much with the separation from your mother. We live in different countries and hardly see each other. I adore you; there is no woman I will ever love more in the world. You are the daughter I always wanted. You are a beautiful and lovely soul. You are gentle and sweet—many virtues you inherited from my former wife.

I would die for you, my daughter. I adore you, I love you, and always will.

To my mum who I adored, and who adored me. Her passing a few years ago left me in a very, very dark place. Tears still come to my eyes when I think or write about her, even now. I miss you, thank you for all the love you gave me. I will always miss you and love you.

To my ex-lover for providing me with the love, support, encouragement, and friendship when I needed it most. I must also thank you for taking it all away, including your friendship, as it inspired me to write it all down, just like you encouraged me to do. I love you, and always will.

To Rachel, my ex-office manager, and ex-office "wife." I remain her Jefe. She was the number one most loyal supporter, colleague, and friend I have ever had. I love you.

To Brian and Janice Muldoon. Brian, thank you for telling me persistently that I had what it took when I thought I was worthless. Thank you for your support. You, Brian, are a smashing man, friend, and coach. I love you.

To Jen Hough, who has come into my life recently to guide me spiritually. With her gift, she has seen through me, what I have experienced, who I am and, most importantly, who I can become and what I can bring to the world. I love you, thank you.

To Emilia work partner in crime, for showing what love is and isn't and for supporting and providing me with love and care when I most needed it, but also for not giving me more than she wanted to offer. Thank you so much too for the help in putting this book together. You've become a true friend. I love you.

A very quick thank you to David Fagan for providing me with some simple but crucial tips to present this book in a way that connected better with readers.

Additional thank you to all of those that have helped me and supported my transition.

INTRODUCTION

As an introduction to this book, I want to honour my mother and honour all mothers. My mum was the first person to probably hold my hand, kiss me, and obviously love me. I adored her, I'll share a few thoughts more about that special love in the love chapter but a book about love without acknowledging the love of a mother or towards a mother will always have something missing.

Before I get into why I wrote this book and where it came from, I also want to be honest and say I have been in pain for a very long time. Due to my circumstances, with my father dying when I was young, I have over the years sought help, advice, and protection from senior colleagues, bosses, partners, and speakers I have promoted.

Jen, my "spiritual coach," as I like to call her, pointed out in one of our coaching sessions that I had been mentally abused for a sustained period. For example, for a period of time, I felt trapped, I was working with a particular trainer whose company and ethics I really didn't enjoy. In fact, I hated the experience. I did it for the higher good of the outcome of the courses and to keep "providing," for my family; but I became increasingly unhappy. I felt so alone for so many years, I wanted to walk away from it all but couldn't.

Has something similar happened to you?

Circumstances and Covid-19 actually allowed me to move away, and now, during the last few years I have been simply trying to heal, explore, share love, follow my calling, and strive to be happy. Writing gives me a sense of joy. I don't want to lay blame anymore for where I am. I am simply a man who wants to take care of myself for once and put myself first instead of others, as I have done all my life.

Hence my openness to discuss vulnerability and love...

Some thoughts about love I have lived or made up, some are generic, and others are more specific. In the process of creating this book—which I like to think of as a heartfelt exploration of the journey of love we bravely undertake in this human existence—I've tapped into my many feelings and emotions and let the keyboard dictate the flow. Sometimes, I have to say, I was pleasantly surprised. At other times the effort aroused no emotion whatsoever. I had never experienced this before. It's also unusual because I consider myself Spanish, but have written many books, including this one, in English. However, many of my thoughts materialise in Spanish. I tend to flow better in Spanish; the words resonate with me more. Therefore, I have written both English and Spanish versions of this book at the same time. There has been so much running through my head, and in several languages, that it's no wonder I have been lost.

Some thoughts are a bit raunchy, as in the "passion" chapter, where I talk about lust, wanting, and spanking, but it's not overdone. Sex is a vital part of what we experience in a relationship as a couple, and we too often shut the door to any conversation about it as though there is something wrong with being a sexual organism. What if we were to celebrate that part of who we are?

I knew I had more in me than what I was seeing when I was at my lowest points, and I suppose that's why I have gone on my journey of self-discovery; my *Ayahuasca* experience definitely influenced me but the opening available through plant medicine is only part of the wisdom I wish to share here. (I'm working on another book that will explore that side of life in more detail, so stay tuned!)

I love every woman who has been in my life. All of them. I will always be there for them. Not only with those I have been intimate with, but also with colleagues who have become friends. I have found them to be such hard workers, committed and loyal, no matter what cause I had at hand. They have all been so loving and caring. I absolutely love women. I say this repeatedly, and mean it in the sincerest, most innocent way possible.

I would stop and put everything on hold to be there for them if they ever needed me, whether trivial or significant, I mean it. I believe love never dies; it simply evolves and transforms.

I shared this story with a very close friend of mine, an east Londoner, born and bred. He worked in Soho all his life. I remember him laughing at me, thinking I had lost it! And what I mean by this is he doesn't understand why I would give up my life in order to stop living a lie, why I would want to explore or elevate my consciousness, in becoming a different and hopefully better human. He would probably label it as a "midlife crisis."

I understand some people will simply not comprehend. I believe "In many ways, we get in our own way." Simply put, it means we are creatures of habit. It means we are not ready to explore or change and I respect that. When we refuse to dive deeper into our consciousness and change our habits, there are so many things we don't know or believe in, because we don't understand. We especially have to look into the behaviours and patterns that are not acceptable, we get in our own way and end up self-sabotaging or regretting. But we've all experienced this, so who am I to judge?

Anyway, getting back to the book. Two books, this one and another, which is nearly finished, entitled *Questioning Love.* The other book is more logical and educational regarding what love means in other cultures, and how it relates to marriage, separation, foreplay, sex, separation, and so on.

It's difficult to write about love. Let me emphasise that, it's very difficult to write about love and more "to be open and express deep feelings around love."

Why is a book like this needed? Well, some thoughts here you may think are very personal to me, but I am trying to tap into humanity's inability to be more open and express what we really feel. My goal is to encourage and inspire more men to wear their hearts on their sleeves and share the love they have with those dear to them.

As I said before in my disclaimer, some parts of the book you may empathise with more than others. Some chapters may feel more aligned, they may activate self-reflection, like falling in love, rejection, or the broken heart section. This is because I let my mind and feelings dictate freely and do not concern myself with how it comes across. With love, my feelings are mine. I am not necessarily a broken man. I have been at certain periods in my life. I am simply happy now to express and share my vulnerability.

You see, as I pointed out, I have learnt that *"love is not what you think it is"* and I don't mean your take on love is necessarily wrong, I mean that love is interpreted differently from person to person. Some people express their love verbally, while others prefer actions to words.

Some prefer to share love with one person; others with multiple people, consecutively or concurrently. Some people prefer to be alone and enjoy friendships instead. Anything goes. *"Love has its ways."*

Whether you are a romantic who likes to express loving thoughts, or love is not your thing, or you have a partner and an open relationship, there is something here for everyone, I hope. However you embrace love, do you delve into it to understand these emotions on a deeper level?

But let me ask you this because I don't have the answer: how would a swinger behave if they exchanged partners every week for several years? I would assume that they still had feelings for their primary partner even though they are sexually engaged with strangers.

Why wouldn't they?

Or how would a partnership that believes in openness and having sex with others react when they break up with their partner?

What if you are someone who doesn't have a partner, only "fuck buddies;" the content in this book would be alien, wouldn't it? Or would it?

It's a question I cannot seem to find the answer because I have not experienced many of those scenarios.

My intention is to engage in both romantic monogamous and open relationships.

Apart from my ex-wife, who was my best friend, and whom I loved very dearly, deeply, and with whom I share many beautiful memories, I had a very passionate love affair for nearly four years with someone I also loved dearly. This woman broke my heart and let me down to some extent. Not because we broke up, which was probably the best for both of us, but because I truly believed we had something special. I thought we were going to remain true friends at least. I'll confess, there was a time I wanted her back. But once the heart is healed, it becomes stronger, like scar tissue on a broken bone. I never tried to rekindle our relationship, but I did tell her I loved and missed her. I think this scared her. And I wonder why I thought we could remain friends? Is it possible for lovers to remain close friends? It must be. Maybe time is all we all need. I'll talk about that.

I am a romantic and fall in love quickly. I am working on becoming less attached, living more in the moment, avoiding the urge to "own or possess anyone," as well as enjoying my life and my own company more. I think the reason I struggle with love is because I fall in love with a woman's soul. As I said, I think women are extraordinary, phenomenal, smart, loving, caring, beautiful creatures. I mean, they can create life!

Lastly, I have written this book because throughout my life I have been loving to a certain degree, but wasn't willing to fully express it. I would hold onto pain and supress my feelings and keep my inner thoughts to myself. It has always been my defense mechanism. I have always had a sense of responsibility - since my dad died when I was 15 - I've always held onto my emotions, dealing with hardship on my own.

Most men are scared to express how they feel and just "bottle it in." Life is short, but life is also beautiful if you embrace it and open up. I still struggle to say what I want to say sometimes, so writing to the people I love is something I do frequently these days.

But let's look at love or loving someone as something we want to do, not something we need to do because we feel alone and a particular person makes us feel good. We tend to associate love with a third party, but love starts from within, it starts with loving yourself and not necessarily with only one person. *You are love, and love has no limits.*

I am a lot more mellow now, but I am also happy to talk about love, express how I feel and have no concerns about what people may think. I can be loving and can also be myself. So, I invite you, men and women, to express your love and embrace whatever form it comes in and let those around you know how you feel. Maybe if you can't say it, you can show it through your actions like quality time or physical touch. Like I said, love has no limits.

And finally, I have experienced love, but I am open for more AND hoping to find a true, lasting love with someone. Will it be monogamous? Maybe, if that's our mutual desire, but I'm happy to keep searching until I do. I believe love is out there for each and every one of us. Only when the time is right though, and with the right person or people.

So here is my heart and soul, served on a plate.

1. LOVE

I have come to this place, wanting to discuss and elevate consciousness about love because life has brought me here. Personal development has become a big part of who I am. Not only because of personal interest but also because I became an international promoter of multiple speakers through my brand The Best You.

On my personal journey, and through these encounters, I realised that love, loving thoughts of love, and ideas were entirely absent from several speakers' talks or subjects.

My separation, followed by my falling in and out of love, and the loss of my mum hit me real hard. Factoring in my age, mortality, experience, and my efforts to find ways to elevate consciousness - more specifically my Ayahuasca experience - I started promoting "The Love Event" and writing two books about love; this one and another due out soon.

Love means many different things to many people. Love is everything, the missing piece in many people's lives. Love is lacking wherever there is conflict, hatred, or despair. It's the big conversation missing at dinner tables, on news stations, in articles and blogs, and amongst colleagues and friends.

Love is so much more than a loving relationship or the love of a sibling. There is divine love, spiritual love, celestial love...

There are many challenges and conflicts in the world, and love is the answer. Love is the only thing that is real.

And having said all that, how can you love anyone else or appreciate love if you don't love yourself? We are lucky to be alive! We have been chosen to be in the here and now; through generations of parents, great parents and great parents, through genetics, chance, and luck.

We are alive, living beings that are all part of higher consciousness, part of this world and everything that lives in it and brought to this world with a purpose. We have to explore what that purpose is.

But it all starts with you, with loving yourself, accepting yourself, and forgiving yourself. Let go of any mistakes you may have made along the way.

I have struggled to forgive myself at times, in letting go. It's only with time that I have accepted myself, with my flaws and no longer seeking anyone's approval but my own, I now feel more complete.

Hopefully, you have had a loving mother who loves you exactly the way you are. Love yourself the same way.

Love yourself for who you are.
Now.

I love myself.

I love who I am.
Because I am who I am
for what I am.

So here I would like to share some thoughts about what love is.
I think...

At a time when
everything seems lost,
and everything
has a cost,
love can sort it all.

At a time
when peace is scarce,
love remains relentless.

Love is the gateway
to every challenge
and adversity
the world is going through.

Love is the first step
towards the last step
and all the steps along the way.

Love breaks all barriers
everywhere,
every time.

Love is the route
to everywhere,
where everything
is possible.

Love is the only thing that is real.

One word that can change the world?
Love.

Love is the route to
everything,
to everywhere,
where anything
can happen.

Small grains of sand can make a dune,
many drops of water can become an ocean,
a few people can become a crowd,
your love can move mountains.

At a time when
everything seems lost,
and everything
has a cost,
your love is always the answer.

Love has the possibility
of breaking down
any impossibility.

The world is sometimes unstable.
Love makes it a safer place.

Obviously, I believe that:

> The hippies and gurus were right.
> The only thing that matters is love.

Unfortunately, we spend our lives pursuing material "things" instead of memories, kindness, and compassion for others.

Trust me, on your deathbed you won't be thinking about who will be wearing your clothes, using your computer, or driving your vehicles. Nope!

You will want to feel love, remember those who loved you, and hopefully leave this world surrounded by love, content in the knowledge that you were loved...

> In the pursuit
> of life's needs,
> we ignore life,
> and life's most
> important need:
> Love.
>
> On your final day,
> with your final breath.
> Love is what you crave,
> love is all you need.
> So why wait?

Love is simply,
yet complexly, everything.

All we want is to be wanted.
All we need is to be needed.
All we love is to be loved.
Love.

The only thing we all need is love,
yet the only thing we struggle to share is love.

Why is love so
difficult to express
when generally, hopefully,
we are born from love?

Some people speak
Others prefer to listen.
Some people choose to ignore
Others prefer to act.
Some people choose hate.
Others prefer to love.
Listen. Act. Love.

Love is not based
on duration
but the intensity
of each moment.

Talking about and sharing thoughts about love with such vulnerability is not something I thought I would ever do. I remember talking to my life coach and questioning why I would pick such a difficult, complex, broad, scary, massive topic as love. Words that a previous mentor of mine shared with me (Sharon Lechter) said to me: If not now, then when, if not you, then who? It made me move forward.

However, my personal troubles and tragedies have expanded my life. Luckily, I have the health and energy to share some of what I've learnt as a result.

But always remember.

> Remember, love never dies,
> it simply transforms.
>
> Remember,
> Love will find a way.

Remember, as I said previously:

> Love is not what
> you think it is.

And

> And if you question love… be careful
> Love only knows how to love.

When you feel down when you don't know what to do…

> One word that can lift you up:
> Love
>
> When in doubt, ask yourself
> what would love do?

I am looking for love. I'm open to talking about and sharing love, so if you find yourself questioning love or you think you haven't got what it takes, that it might be too late for you. Remember that love can be displayed in a variety of ways: random acts of kindness, volunteer work, donations, compliments... the list goes on.

All is Love:

> Love does not understand age,
> time or gender,
> all it does is surrender.
> It's love.

Love is like the sun,
sometimes you don't see or feel it,
but it's always there.

You have to trust love
because love is the only thing
worth trusting.

If you let love do what it does best
you won't have to worry about the rest.

You are matter, I am matter.
Love is the only word that matters.

Love is the place
where everything
is possible.

Some questions for you:

Is love the most important thing in your life?

Do you feel loved?

Can you share some love right now?

If so, with whom? Do it. Why wait?

Who has loved you unconditionally? Let them know what this has meant to you.

What does love mean to you? Write three thoughts down.

Do you share love? If so, in what way? Write it down.

Fall in Love with... (fill in the blank).

2. FALLING IN LOVE.

Let me start by opening this chapter in dedication to my mum. The first woman who I ever loved, and fell in love with. The woman who loved me unconditionally, always.

How can anyone love you more than your mother? It's difficult because it is unconditional and eternal.

Losing my mum made me lose it. I adored my mum. She was so strong, amazing, a real woman. I love all Aries signsbecause of my mum. They are special, loving people with an amazing temperament and fiery personalities. Some very basic words to express the eternal, celestial, galactic love I have for my mum are dedicated below.

To My Mum

A character, a personality,
wise, brave and loyal with ample humility.

Her strength and bravery were inspiring,
her generosity never tiring.

Her smile, beauty and tenderness would melt you,
and those black eyes would convert you.

She was sweet like honey,
she was such a character,
she had great humour and was very funny.

She lived, she explored,
and by everyone adored.

She was strong, honest
all her life, living it to the fullest.

My heart is now broken.
Life will never be the same.
But moving forward, I will live my life the same,
with plenty of passion,
to live up to your fame.

I love you mum.
The end.

I touch my skin
to feel you.
I look into my eyes
to see you.

I am you,
I am part of you.
I miss you mum.

Your love for me was infinite,
I wish I had told you more often
how much I loved you,
and how much you meant,
it will always be my regret.
I love you and still feel you around.
Thank you, you beautiful soul,
you are in my daily thoughts,
will continue to remain there
until I am deep in the ground.

What a beautiful feeling of falling in love. Maybe you've been lucky enough to be in love with your "boy or girl" all your life, or maybe you have experienced many.

For those of us who are looking for love, "falling in love" is a beautiful stage of our experience.

But before we do, let's talk about what falling in love is and review what it might not be!

Sexual chemistry, loving someone's touch, the tenderness of their hand, the warmth of their lips. The electricity when your tongues intertwine, their warm hand when it touches your body, the connection you feel, the closeness when you are intimate, or the blissful sex—it's all wonderful but not necessarily the same as "falling in love."

It might be confusing. *You simply love the experience of being with that person* or love the sex and how it makes you feel. Maybe you don't know how long it will last, maybe you care or maybe you don't. My advice is to enjoy it.

> For it to be more,
> you both need to
> understand if it *is* more.
>
> You can love,
> and feel love
> with someone
> who is not meant
> to be a lover.

Sometimes, people simply come into your life to teach you what love is not!

She came into my life to teach me
what I didn't know about love.

Some people will come
into your life to
teach you that not everyone
you love is worth loving.

Love can be
simple,
short,
beautiful,
passionate,
and memorable.

Every love story
is different,
thank God they are.
If not,
life would
be rather boring.

Not everyone is the one. You don't "have to fall in love" with everyone. There is a lesson in everything.

Not every love story
is "the love story."

You should know
that not every frog
you kiss is the
prince or princess.

For those of us out there looking for love, "falling in love" is a beautiful phase of experience. Sometimes we go mad, we do "illogical" but beautiful things- we follow the heart!

How scary, how exciting when...

> I knew in a heartbeat
> my heart was yours.
>
> I knew in a heartbeat
> your heart was mine.

One of my flaws is that I love women. I see beauty in all of them. Sometimes I tend to fall in love too quickly because I see their soul, their love, their heart and I feel connected. I don't necessarily look at appearances, it's more their energy that attracts me.

Maybe you have fallen in love many times, or you are one of those who falls in love instantly...

Falling in love with her was easy,
it happened instantly
effortlessly.

I looked at her
She looked at me
We knew
The Beginning.

I fell in love with you before I met you
because you were always in my dreams.

How can I explain
what I felt the first time
I saw you?
Love.

How can I explain
what I felt the first time
I saw you?
I lost all my senses.

That sense of floating in the air, or that beautiful feeling of butterflies in your belly.

Stop and remember, remember the time, go there...

On my way to see you,
birds sing,
the sun shines,
butterflies fly.
Bliss.

The wind blows
the waves stroke the shores
the birds sing
the sun shines
I am yours.
Bliss

Or remember those times when all you can do is think of her or him, you can't focus and all you want to see is their face. You keep texting and sending love messages, you can't focus. All you see is her or him.

Just like the stars need the space within space,
every day I need to see your beautiful face.

The stars
and the immensity
of space
cannot compare
to how beautiful I see
your stunning face.

What a difference
a day makes
and the difference
is you.

It's that phase of falling in love, transitioning to a true love, when you least expect it or maybe when you actually aren't looking for it.

You are still not 100% that she or he is the one, but you love the buzz. You are floating, you are love, you ooze love, you are glowing.

Sometimes when you are simply
loving what you do,
loving who you are,
not looking for love…
Love knocks at your door.
It's love, it's what it does.

I was looking for where I wanted to live,
and suddenly without wanting to,
I found with whom I would want to live.

Love comes your way sometimes
when you least expect it,
kind of when you go out on a summer's night,
in shorts and flip-flops and
you get soaked by a summer storm.
It just came out of nowhere.

Sometimes the wind blows too hard,
sometimes there is no wind.
Like love, the wind will come and go.
Enjoy the sail while you can.

A thousand love songs
with a thousand lyrics
is what I need to express
how much I love you.

I can't love you and not love you.
And I mean wanting you close,
seeing you, feeling you,
touching you and holding you.

Now
I'm lost.
Lost in your love.

Some questions for you:

Do you believe in falling in love?

Do you think it's attraction first, then you might fall in love?

If you've fallen in love with a friend?

What was it that made it change from friendship love to romantic love?

If you have someone you have loved for a long time.

Are you still falling in love with them? If you are, are you expressing it?

Are you letting them know? Do it now.

What is falling in love like for you? Write three things down about what it is for you. What is it?

How would you describe it?

And what is it? Why are you falling in love? You don't under-stand, well you do know... It's the attraction.

3. ATTRACTION

Where does all this falling in love come from?
Why are we attracted to one another?
Personality, humour, looks, smells, eyes, hands, and body obviously play a big role in determining our desires. Whatever the reason, we become attracted.
For me, and many, knowingly or unknowingly, it's the energy.
You can't help it; you can't fight it.

How beautiful, just to let go.

> Your energy was the gravity
> that brought me to you.
>
> Your energy is your gravity,
> which I find impossible to ignore.
> It's physics, it's physical,
> it's so much more.

Sometimes it's "just" a physical attraction. You just can't control it, and why would you anyway? Live the life you have been given.

Real attraction
is unstoppable,
unquestionable,
and unbelievable.
Let it be.

I was attracted to you.
The End. The Beginning.

I was attracted to you
one late afternoon,
instantly,
relentlessly,
constantly,
helplessly,
like the sun attracts the Earth,
and the Earth attracts the moon.

She was born with this
capacity to turn men or women on,
for them to lose their senses.
It's so much more than
attraction, there are just no defences.
Surrender.

Men and women
are attracted to her.
She can't help it.
Why would she?

I was attracted to you.
It was the beginning!

While you can try to control it, you want to unreel those images in your mind, ones you can share with your lover but would rather make a reality.

Wouldn't you? Of course, why wouldn't you?

Attraction,
Hard, intense,
physical attraction
is like a wild animal;
it can't be tamed.
Well, it can, but in only one way.

Some people are born attractive
in personality, not necessarily looks.
They charm and attract you,
and in your mind,
you surrender yourself.

He had a magnetism
that attracted the living,
and woke the dead.

She walks around
with this spellbinding
sexual appeal that is
impossible not to find attractive.
Sex appeal.

Let your attraction loose, find the prey,
and once you get them, don't let go.
It doesn't matter how much they pray.

You drive me crazy,
you drive me wild.
I can't wait to have you
undressed by my side.

And that attraction can be overwhelmingly strong, forcing you to think they are the one. You're sold. You want them, right there, right now.

And you don't want to let go.

> I am attracted to you
> like clouds to the sky,
> birds to the air,
> bees to the flower.
> I want you now and I just don't care.
>
> Your body to me
> is a sexy,
> hot magnet.
> Like the Earth to the moon,
> you are my planet.
>
> What attracted me to her
> was not so much
> her smile
> or her amazing beauty.
> It was her calmness,
> her intelligence.
> To share time with her
> and be her companion
> was my only duty.
>
> They say,
> "Let the music play,"
> but to me
> "playing with you"
> is like music.

You make me want
to achieve new heights.
You have that rain that
makes everything in me grow.

This was meant to be,
it is what it is,
and will be what will be,
you will see.
But for me, it's not enough.
I want more.

I do hope you forgive me for saying this,
but just looking at your lips,
I wonder what the rest of you tastes like.

I don't have a dirty mind,
I just have an imagination
where I do all sorts of sexual
things to you.

You are sexy,
sensual,
fiery,
hot,
sheer excellence.
You excite me to points
where I have no reference.

My questions to you:

What do you find attractive in a partner?

What is it that really excites you about them?

Have you told him or her? Told them enough? Tell them now!

What's not physical about a partner that attracts you?

Describe attraction in three ways.

This attraction is burning wild, continuously building up intensity. It was meant to be a few encounters, or maybe only one. You never saw it coming, or maybe your intention was not to let it become serious - but it's going to escalate into something beautifully complicated, beautifully passionate.

4. PASSION

The simple act of kissing, that beautiful connection where two kiss and you become one, perfectly in sync. A place where souls and hearts connect. I think if you find a good kisser, you will always remember them and cherish those very special moments.

Who doesn't love kissing a good kisser?

> Kissing is the door
> to everything
> and so much more.

> You left me a few hours ago.
> I am still licking my lips
> to taste yours.

> First of all, let me tell you I think you look divine,
> and I don't know if we are going to be
> in each other's lives for a while
> or for a long time.
> But tonight, I intend to kiss you,
> love you passionately and make you mine.

Then the passion hits you. You dismiss doubt and let go of your senses and fantasies. There is no logic, and very little sense. So, who cares! You just let go.

I believe passion starts with the fantasies that materialise in your mind. As part of the build-up, share your thoughts with your lover, detail what you would like, to do to them, with them, and follow through with it....

It's such a magnificent adventure!

> Sorry,
> but I did not ignite it.
> You will be mine,
> don't fight it.
> Lust.
>
> I have to let you know
> "completely inappropriate thoughts about you"
> occupy my mind every day.
>
> When I see you, I get horny.
> When I touch you, I go mad.
> What a beautiful adventure.

Start all over again.

I want you,
and I want you now.
You won't be able to resist,
just like the sun needs to shine.
I need you to be mine
because only together can we exist.

I want you in ways
that cannot be
expressed in words,
but needs to be tested.
If people knew what I was thinking,
I would probably be arrested.

I want you in every room,
everywhere,
always.

I want you,
I need you now,
don't give me excuses,
come with me,
and find out how.

I have explained what I think,
and perhaps for you it is very intense.
But I don't know how to express myself
any other way.
I need you by my side, here and now.
That's what I feel,
that's the only thing that makes any sense.

I cannot think.
I do not care.
The moment you get close to me,
I am in despair.

Not sure what you have done to me,
but the moment you get close,
blood pumps between my legs.

My heart beats in your proximity.
You're driving me mad.
You're playing with my sanity.

Sometimes, you can't control it.
Sometimes, you don't want to control it.
Sometimes, you are so happy you didn't.
Sometimes, you have to try or die inside.

When they surrender their body to you, you become the researcher for that teasing, sexy body.

You take this job very seriously, become an expert in that amazing body you have been permitted to explore.

You are the perfect person for the job.

> You,
> you are my favourite dish.
> forget any vegetable,
> meat or fish.
> I Love Eating you.
>
> My hands know every single
> curve of your magnificent body,
> yet when I end,
> I question if I have left any inch untouched,
> and I am forced
> to re-examine
> at every opportunity I have.
>
> Every curve is a blessing.
> One of my favourite things
> to do to you
> is all that undressing.

She surrenders her body,
soul and mind
because she knows
she is about to feel divine!

She surrendered,
she knew
what he was pursuing,
and she also knew
that he knew
what he was doing.

He took control of her
in ways that only he had permission.

Enjoy that body,
don't leave an inch unexplored,
kissed and adored.

With permission granted, you let your imagination go wild. Something ignites within you, where your inner animal takes over, and you desperately want to do things to them as soon as possible, as often as possible and in as many ways as possible.

The thing is I love it,
you bring the bad out in me.

When she's good, she's bad.
When she's really bad, she's even better.

It didn't matter what he had planned,
she was ready for whatever
he brought on, and so much more.

He wants her,
he needs her,
his insatiable thirst for her has no end,
firmly and wildly,
he is going to make her bend and bend.

I want you so badly, it's a disgrace.
When I have you,
you will lose your mind,
all sense of time and space,
our bodies will become one,
beautifully intertwined.

You dirty girl!
You left your hand
and finger marks
when I had you
in front of the mirror.
I can't get my head around cleaning it.

We were so close,
as close as you can get.
But pulling your hair firmly towards me
made us one, and for that wild moment,
there was nothing you could do,
you were all mine.
The Mirror.

I am not spanking you
as a punishment,
I am spanking you
as a reward.

It's difficult to describe, isn't it? But when it all ends, you want it to start all over again. When is enough, enough?

How can you describe to the blind
how amazing
it is to wake up the next morning
after an intense night
and I made you mine?

Your moist and fleshy lips excite me,
get me hot and horny.
I lose control again and again.
All I want is to have you
and not let go
until the sun rises, and only then.

Your lips kiss me,
I heat up.
Your hands touch me,
I get excited.
You give me your body,
I ascend.

You are lust,
unbridled passion.
I want to do everything to you
because I can and must.
You always manage to release me from my sadness.
I don't care about anything when I'm with you,
and together I want to embrace this beautiful madness.

Some questions for you:

What does passion mean to you?

Are you vocal or descriptive with your partner about what you enjoy?

Are you holding back in the passion department?

What could you do to let go?

What have you learnt? Write it down.

Write down three ways you would like to spice it up?

Describe three passionate scenes for you? Can you share them? Have you shared them?

What drives you mad about them?

Maybe those sparkling, mysterious eyes and the way they look at you?

5. EYES

I find eyes fascinating. I tend to look deeply into people's eyes. You can see so much more than the colour. Look beyond those adoring eyes at every opportunity.

Eyes can show you their journey...

> From what I have seen
> in your eyes,
> I can see the pain,
> the joy,
> happiness,
> and the love you have to give,
> and everything in between.

Eyes can break through barriers, open hearts, melt you to your core, and leave you defenceless.

Your eyes are bottomless wells
that connect with my soul.
You are deep in my cells.

I got lost in her eyes
and never wanted to be found.
I disappeared into her arms,
and for the first time, I felt alive.
And when I kissed her sweet lips,
I instantly knew I was bound.

I am defenceless
when you look at me
with those loving eyes.
Senseless.

Your eyes make me feel
safe when I'm lost,
wanted when I feel undesired,
and looked at when not seen.

Looking into your eyes
is like looking into eternity.

In the twinkling of an eye,
I fell in love.

Is it the colour of their eyes?

I love you, love your eyes.

Your black eyes
are deep and dark,
so, it's difficult to understand
how looking into them
reveals your soul so clearly,
and how they light up my heart.

Your eyes are bright and blue,
So, it's easy to understand
how looking into them
reveals your soul so clearly,
how they bring light to my heart.

I can see the forest,
the trees,
your eyes are magnetic,
they make my heart freeze.
So mesmerising, so green,
they need to be seen
to be believed.

How about when you look into those eyes and see their soul?
Has that happened to you? It's this deep sense of connection.

You may think our eyes
have never met,
but if you look deeply,
you will see easily
that this is something
we have done in a life before,
and something
we should never forget.

Eyes are not only for seeing,
they are to be seen as
they are the doors to the soul.

I'm happy.
I'm lost.
I'm lost in your eyes.
I can see your soul….

I have a question.
I hope you can make me understand.
When our eyes connect,
what do you see?
What do you feel?
Because to me, it seems
we go far and beyond
to another land in another world.

I think this is a sign.
I can see your soul through
your eyes.
You can see mine?

If eyes are the doors to one's soul,
you, my love, have the keys.

Does anything compare to the feeling when someone looks at you with love?

Oh, I love that! I love to be looked at with love.

> Your eyes guide me,
> your eyes calm me,
> your eyes balm me,
> your eyes are soothing,
> your eyes are oozing,
> your eyes are stunning,
> your eyes are beautiful,
> and so are you.
>
> Your eyes are pools
> of joy, happiness
> and comfort,
> At one and the same time.
> And right now,
> I can see them
> wanting you to make
> you mine.

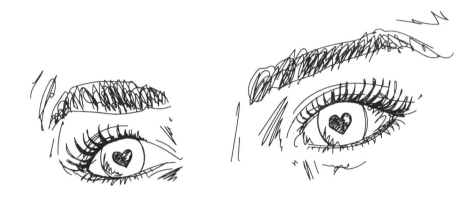

When you look at me
with your loving eyes,
I feel I have everything I need
and more,
everything that it implies.

If you are lucky enough
for her to look at you
with her loving eyes,
you have been blessed,
and all your hopes and desires
forever have been addressed.

I got lost in your eyes.
Don't come
looking for me.
Happy place.

Some questions for you:

What do you find extraordinary about eyes?

Do you look deeply into your partner's eyes?

What do they mean to you when you see them? Write them down.

It's not only the eyes, it's her. It's her I love and want for so many reasons....

6. SHE

She is special, she is perfect, every little quirk, every little movement, the way she strokes her hair, her warmth, her voice, the way she bites her fingernail when she's nervous....

She knows what she wants and will warn you.

> She told him:
> I am easy to want,
> difficult to forget.

She...

> She didn't have to think much.
> She loved him instantly.
>
> She was easy to love,
> impossible to forget.
>
> She was easy to love,
> difficult to un-love,
> impossible to hate.

She was the one
who kept him
dreaming all-day
and awake at night.

She is fresh like the breeze,
and comes to you at ease.
She's good on the eye,
the dream of every guy.

She is asleep…
When she wakes up,
the sun will shine,
the earth will spin,
the moon will glow,
the birds will sing.
Just wait and see.

But before we delve into her, what about you? Are you prepared?

Are you man enough? Can you give her the love she needs?

Some boys think they are ready when they are not. Some men with all their wisdom will fall short.

It requires a real man
who embraces her exactly the way she is,
and wouldn't change a thing.

She didn't need a boy. She needed a man!
She will have days when she needs space.
She will have days when she questions everything.
She will need a man who gives her space when needed.
She will need a man who loves her when she craves affection.
She will need a man who can put her at ease.
And one day, she might not want any of it.
Be prepared.

He fed her love,
when suddenly
she realised
she had never eaten.

To him, she is a goddess,
and as a goddess,
she needs to be
revered,
admired,
and adored.

Yes, it's difficult to describe why you chose her. There are so many things about her you like, what would be the words?

> Words made a vague attempt
> to describe what she is,
> but basically, words could not find words.

But what was it about her? So many things, so many....

Asleep you are beautiful,
awake you are divine.
For me, you have everything.
Your beauty makes me crazy,
you are everything that is fine.

Resistance is futile,
be prepared to be assimilated
by her love.

I don't remember
life without her.
I couldn't see,
it was dark.
She brought me
the light.

The best day of my life
was the day she looked
at me with loving eyes!

Her stride is full of purpose,
firm and steady,
fast and slow,
confident and always ready.

What would love say?
Love her!

Once she puts a spell on you,
it's game over.

She is the kind
of woman who
makes you see instantly
what's been missing
all your life.

Was it her smile? I believe anything can happen.
Anyone, even the toughest men,
will melt with a beautiful smile.

She had me with her smile.

> It took no time,
> not even a while.
> It was instant.
> It was her smile.

> Her look strikes your soul,
> her smile drills a hole.

> What makes her special?
> The softness of her hand,
> the tenderness of her touch,
> the warmth of her heart,
> the vastness of her eyes,
> the light in her smile.

> Her smile
> is all he needed!

The way she kissed? We talked about kissing and connecting before. Let's not forget the kissing.

> A kiss is a kiss.
> Well, I suppose it depends
> if she kissed your lips
> or kissed your heart.

> A kiss is a kiss.
> Well, I suppose it depends
> if she kissed your lips
> or kissed your soul.

Her body is the beautiful vessel her soul is travelling in, the one you adore and spend your days dreaming about and nights exploring.

What a beautiful thing a woman's body is. How magnificent.

Her body was his temple,
her curves his excitement,
her lips a place called home,
her taste sweet as honey.

I'm drawn to drawing
every curve
in that magnificent body
of yours.

Her curves were
like the French Riviera,
exciting to drive,
amazing to look at.

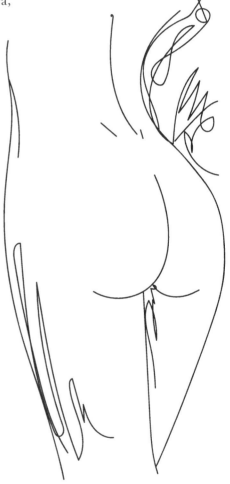

She had these amazing
long legs that you couldn't
help gawking at.
Luckily,
I could look at them all day
if I wanted,
and God I wanted.

If legs were measured in days,
hers would be measured in weeks.

Is it that personality? Maybe she is soft and sweet, or fiery with a short temper, or witty with a wicked sense of humour. Maybe she has all those virtues and more, and you find everything about her adorable. Maybe she has them all... You are a lucky beast, and you know it.

> If you want to hold a rose,
> sometimes you will
> have to put up with the thorns.
>
> She has a temper
> that is difficult to tame.
> That's what defines her,
> and you want her all the same.
>
> Sometimes she has
> her "moments,"
> sometimes she's a bit clumsy.
> In his eyes, these "imperfections" are
> what makes her so adorable.
>
> You are gorgeous,
> smart and pretty.
> Your sense of humour
> is witty,
> and I can't wait
> to travel the world with you,
> visit every city.

Is it maybe the way she dresses? She looks stunning no matter what she wears —yoga pants, jeans, heels, and those sexy dresses.

> She looks amazing in any attire or dress,
> yet she is so much better to undress.

Home is defined as the place where you store your belongings. The place you live is not home. Who needs a home when it's empty, soulless, with no one to share it? SHE is home, nothing else compares, nothing. She is home. Home any day of the week.

Home is her arms, her hands, her warmth, her sweetness, her cuteness, and her love....

I don't care if right now I am alone.
I never am
because I can always go back to her,
and she is home.

What was she like?
She was home.
A place you wanted to stay
and never leave, and even when you did,
you always wanted to return.

What was she like?
She was like home, like being at home
on a Sunday morning.

The lust? Are you just a hot and horny individual or does she make you that way? You feel aroused when you are simply next to her. No one else makes you feel that way. Right?

She wants him, constantly.
He wants her everywhere.

She is fire and spice,
and everything that is nice.

She was very gifted with her tongue,
and she wasn't a speaker!

She was very gifted
with her lips,
and they weren't only
for kissing.

Her honey is sweet,
and he was her bumble bee.

Her beauty makes you behave bad.
Not having her makes you go mad.

Having her was everything.

When she walks into the room,
air becomes lighter.
And sorry to be crude,
his pants will likely become tighter.

They say the girl plays with your mind,
and the woman plays with your body.
They say the girl plays with your mind,
and the woman explores it.

I did warn you, and as someone said, love stories end in trag-edy. One day, she will probably fly away.

> What you have to understand about her
> is that at some point, she will move on.
> Because she needs to explore,
> to feel,
> to love.
> And hopefully, she will
> remember and miss you in the process.
>
> You can fight.
> But sometimes you have to let go.
>
> Take it on the chin…

She's gone. You still have beautiful memories...and your last wishes would be what?

> When was my life complete?
> When I had her.
>
> God asked:
> What would you like to see for the last time?
> Her smile, he replied.
> God asked:
> What would you like to feel for the last time?
> Her touch, he replied.
> God asked:
> What would you like to taste for the last time?
> Her lips, he replied.
>
> She was the one who got away.
>
> He fell in love when he didn't want to.
> She fell out of love when
> he didn't want her to.

Questions for you:

What is it about her? Write it down.

Physically?

Emotionally?

Spiritually?

Have you told her?

When was the last time you told her?

Do you want to tell her now?

What about him? What is it about him?

7. HE

He is special. Everything about him you love. He's sexy, funny, witty, and smart.

What was it about him? What does he have those other men don't have, can't have, won't have?

He did warn her, too:

>He told her:
>I am easy to want,
>difficult to forget.

He knew:

>He didn't have to think much.
>He loved her, instantly.

What makes him different? Is he passionate, is he loving, does he have a great personality? Does he have a way of loving you unlike anyone before? Is it the way he loves you?

He was easy to love,
impossible to forget.

He seemed crazy
but he was only
crazy in love.

He seemed crazy,
but he was only
crazy in love.
Crazy for the touch
of her hand,
her lips,
her love.

He didn't know how
to love her any other way,
just all the way.

He was the one
who kept her
daydreaming
and awake at night.

He didn't need much,
her smile
and her love
were plenty.
Having her
was happiness intently.

He didn't just love her,
he adored her.
You see, he believes
adoration is a
higher form of love.

At a time when
love seemed scarce,
he had an abundance of love to give.

If he had one flaw,
it was that he loved
too intensely.

The best day of my life
was the day he looked
at me with loving eyes!

What would love say? Love him!

If love is air,
he provided
all the air
she would ever need.

To him,
it was her.

But what was it about him? Well, he liked his woman exactly the way that she was, he adored everything about her because he knew that:

> Changing a perfect woman
> requires the imperfect man

Was it his smile?

> His smile
> was all he needed!
>
> He had this smart, casual,
> confidence about himself.
> His sexy style was irresistible
> with his beautiful smile.

Is it the way he speaks to you?

> He speaks to her
> like no one had ever done before.
> His words filled with unfamiliar adoration.
>
> He speaks to her
> like no one had ever done before.
> His words dirty and lustful all at once.
>
> His voice is sexy.
> His voice is horny.
> With the added pretences,
> it brings out sexuality.
> It's a beautiful new reality
> that enhances her senses.
>
> His words touched her soul,
> the way the sun's rays bathe the sea,
> with beauty and reflection.

Is it how he touches you?

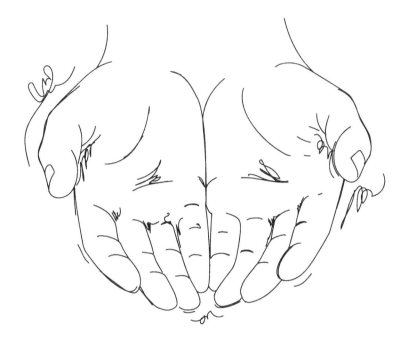

His fingers and hands
knew every part of her body,
yet he was happy to explore
it again and again.

He had strong hands.
He was ready
and able to hold
her in ways
she had never
been held before.

Is it how he turns you on? Is it his sexuality? Maybe it's his sex appeal?

He will walk into the room,
and she will feel his presence.
In her mind, you can assume
she runs through
the passion, lust and in essence,
everything she would like him to get into.

He was very gifted with his tongue,
and he wasn't a speaker!

He was very gifted
with his lips,
and it wasn't only
for kissing.

He did things to her
that needed trying.
She loved it so much,
her joy had her crying.

Maybe it's his confidence?

> Once upon a time,
> as they looked at each other
> from the other side of the room,
> he walked towards her
> and whispered in her ear:
> "I want you and need you to
> hold my hand and let's go…"
> And off they went.
> The end… and the beginning

He was a hard worker in bed because his love deserved all the pleasure she could handle on repeat. He loved loving her.

> He loved loving her.

> He took control of her
> in ways only he had permission.

> He touched her in ways
> she had never been touched before.
> For the first time
> "she felt what it is to feel."

> He spanked her hard,
> not because she was bad
> but because she was good.

He was home. A hug, holding hands, his soothing voice, the way he took care of her, cooked for her, loved her and adored her... it all meant home! It was all she needed.

> She listens to him
> because his voice
> is like music,
> his voice is home.
>
> When he held her, she knew
> she could feel
> no other place
> in the world she would rather be.
> He was home, it's all she ever wanted.
>
> She had travelled far,
> met some people along the way
> and over the years.
> But suddenly
> in the middle of nowhere
> with his arms around her,
> she knew she was home.

Questions for you:

What is it about him? Write it down.

Physically?

Emotionally?

Spiritually?

Have you told him?

When was the last time you told him?

Do you want to tell him now?

Next step now... we want to keep this alive. We are in Love.

8. IN LOVE

Okay, so LOVE is in the air. We are deeply in love. We love each other's company. We feel entwined - a home to each other, and we don't want to leave. The world does not exist. It's just the two of us!

It's beautiful living happily with someone you love, someone you want, where "everything clicks." It doesn't happen easily. Sometimes, it's better to be alone if you are not with someone you deeply love. But when you do, is there anything else quite like it?

I don't think so. I have been lucky enough to experience it a few times. It's a beautiful place. When you are in love, the simple things are what make it so special. Maybe the way she or he, hugs you, holds you. It's simple, special and spiritual, you feel safe.

> The way you hug me, hold me,
> it's what holds me together.

You wouldn't change a thing. Not one thing, as far as you are concerned, she is perfect, you're perfect.

> You are
> the
> perfect
> imperfection.
>
> You are
> my
> perfect
> imperfection.

This love feels so intense, so beautiful.

You are delicate and divine.
You are beautiful.
I love that you are mine.

There is nothing more beautiful
than to wake up in the morning
and see those magnificent
curves of yours and the
stunning beauty of your face.

Love is not complicated, it's simple.
The key is
communication,
but also holding hands,
a cuddle,
kissing,
and having meaningful
conversations.

My heart is yours,
and yours is mine.
Who cares about anything else?

Loving you is like breathing.
It's impossible for me to stop.

What was it that made it CLICK? It seems right, like it was always meant to happen.

> One day,
> luckily,
> beautifully,
> you walked
> into my life.
>
> You know when
> something is meant to be.
> It just is.
>
> I knew you were out there.
> I just hadn't found you yet.
>
> I am not sure what it was.
> I simply knew.
> I knew that I knew nothing
> but I was about to learn everything.
> Love.

I've been alive for many years.
I woke up the day I found you.
The moment I saw you,
everything made sense.
Until then, I was living
a senseless life.
Awake.

I've driven along thousands of roads.
I only want to drive on
the ones that lead me to you.

I come from a place
where the bitter is sweet,
the angry are happy,
the poor are rich and
hate is compassion.
It's called your heart.

I belong to you,
you belong to me.
The End. The Beginnig.

Love is not mathematical.
If it was,
you,
plus me,
that would equal happiness.

I've talked about hands several times in the book. Hands are capable of so much, to stroke, tickle, warm, build, create, grab, to hold.

Not sure what it means to you, but how beautiful it is to find the perfect hands to hold. People have been holding hands for thousands of years; it's an expression of love, of feeling safe, of making your partner feel safe.

Think about how special it is when your hands slide in and connect "perfectly." Isn't it one of the most beautiful loving things about being in love?

Don't take it for granted. It's a beautiful way of feeling and showing love. It makes you both feel safe... Not everyone deserves to hold your hand, remember that.

As I write these words I think of my mum and how she was probably the first one to hold my hand. I think of the women I have loved, and how I loved holding all their hands, my daughter when she was small, and soon hopefully my grandkids.

We all want to have someone special holding our hand in our final days, don't we?

When her fingers
connect with yours
and your hands link
it all makes sense.

Like kissing,
holding hands,
It's special, it's my well-being.
When it happens it is magical,
extraordinary, wonderful,
It's one of the most magnificent
things about being a human being.

In those seconds when your fingers
fit with mine in a natural way
when our hands become one.
Suddenly, as if nothing else, I feel divine,
it's supernatural, not much more I can say.

Your hand holding mine
is all I wish for.
I adore.
Because at that moment,
nothing worries me,
nothing disturbs me,
nothing fazes me,
nothing frightens me anymore.

Hands, hearts and souls
that are meant
to connect will connect.
Connect
naturally,
instinctively,
inexplicably.

I've travelled far,
far and beyond,
in planes, ships,
done thousands of miles
across the land
and it looks like all that I needed
was for you to hold my hand.

You know when it feels so right, you are so ecstatic and grateful to have her in your life. What is it about the way they love you? They sense things, they seem to know you better than yourself. Why does it feel so right?

How can I not love you?
If something happens to me, you can feel it
If I'm in pain, you heal me
If when I'm sad, you feel me
If I need the truth, you reveal it
How can I not love you?

I can't describe it.
It's *"the way you love me"*
that I love so much.

I only know to love you.

I have this deep
and unstoppable
desire to write,
to tell the world
how much I love you.

What about when you lay in bed together? You "spoon each other." You feel their warm body next to yours; you hug each other; you become one, perfectly intertwined, your legs tied together; there is nowhere in the world you would rather be. You feel safe there.

You know what I mean.

> Feeling your body,
> your warm body next to mine,
> where we become one,
> for me, it's the most divine.
> Nothing compares.
> It gives me peace,
> It makes me feel safe,
> It calms me down,
> it's everything,
> I have no cares.
>
> If I have a nightmare
> or insomnia takes over
> to find you in bed,
> being able to touch you
> It soothes me,
> it calms me,
> It quiets my head.

You feel taller, younger, smarter, and more fulfilled. Complete.

I write with my heart
because my head
does not know how to write.
Logic and analytics
can never do you justice.
They won't get it right.

The moment I fell in love with you,
everything was right,
everything made sense.
I became fearless, relentless.
Flying in the clouds high like a kite.

You feel lost without each other!

When I'm alone,
my mind is with you.

I still feel close to you,
even from a distance.

Loving you from a distance
is not easy, but love will find a way.

If I am not there or you can't find me,
just look inside your heart.

When I fly,
I feel closer to you.
Heaven.

Please keep in mind
that you are always
on my mind.

I miss you,
long for you,
yearn for you,
the bottom line is
I adore you.

Is this forever? It seems like it, you believe so!

Your love is mine and mine is yours,
just like the water looks for the shores.

It was only a question of time.
Together.

If I live a hundred lives,
I would want you in all of them.

If I could choose
a place to die,
it would be in your arms.

If heaven
is what we all aspire to,
I don't want it
unless you are there with me.

Happiness comes from having you
and what I always wanted.
Loving you.

Three easy words to say,
impossible for some.
I love you.

There are times I don't know what to say,
with all the love I have for you
because I am
struggling
to focus my thoughts.
What I want is your permission
to love you more
and not go through so much suffering.

I overthink and think of you
nonstop.
I'm obsessed,
possessed.
It's jealousy and love and it doesn't have
any logic, I know.
It's a profanity,
but what can I do
if I have lost my sanity?

I shared previously that I believe adoration is a higher form of love. It's when an "I Love You" falls short to describe what you feel for your lover. You adore him or her.

> Having you,
> holding you,
> feeding you,
> hugging you,
> kissing you,
> caring for you,
> touching you,
> caressing you,
> comforting you,
> listening to you,
> looking at you,
> satisfying you,
> loving you,
> for me,
> it's all summed up in two words.
> Adoring You
>
> I don't know how to respond to so much passion,
> that's why my heart
> is disoriented, in a state of confusion,
> because I love you,
> I adore you.
> I've lost my mind, that's my conclusion.

Was it meant to be? Are our souls connected?

Your amazing body is simply a vessel
for your beautiful soul.
A soul that has been
connected to mine
and has travelled
far and beyond
between lives
to connect now
in this time.

Yes, we have met before.
Our love has been eternal
and has travelled through
time and space.
So now, right now,
we can continue
what will always be continued.

Our Eternal Love.

Their souls have been together
in previous lives.
He knows, she knows.
This unstoppable,
uncontrollable,
animalistic
desire cannot
be controlled or tamed.
They both succumb
to pleasure and love.

Destiny

My questions to you:

What does being in love mean to you? Write three thoughts down.

Have you shared them with your partner?

How many times do you tell her you love her?

Is saying *I love you* enough? How else would you express it? Do you agree with me that adoring is a higher form of love? What do you adore about her? Write it down. Have you told your partner?

What loving things can your hands do today?

Who needs to feel the warmth and strength of your hands?

What loving words can you write down and who can you share it with?

Write it down.

Loving you is...

I adore you because...

Holding your hand means...

So much love. Everlasting love. I'm crazy but only crazy in love with YOU!

I appreciate some of you, some of us may not have a person to share our loving thoughts with or someone to hold your hand at this moment. You will, when you do, share it, tell them, let them feel the love, your love.

9. YOU

Hey, you! Yes, you. There are so many great things about you. As far as I am concerned, you have it all, no one compares! I look at no one. No one could ever give me the love you give me, or have given me. Yes, there are attractive people out there, but they are not you, it's all about you.

If, at the time of reading this, YOU are not special to someone, let me tell you, YOU are amazing. The planet holds eight billion people. Let them see how beautiful you are.

When I am in love, all I want is YOU.

I want YOU

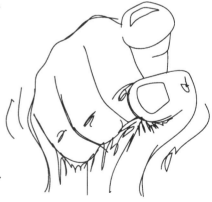

> I have this
> insatiable thirst
> for you.
>
> Time (it was only a matter of).

Like wine, you get better with age.
You have an amazing body and scent.
The more I taste you, the more I want you.

YOU are all I need.

You are what I need.
I need what you are.

You are the first thing
I think about in the morning.
Every morning.

You are the last thing
I think about at night.
Every night.

You.
That's it.

You are my air,
the rest I don't care.

The meaning of life
is to love.
My life's meaning
is to love you.

If I had to say something,
it's that you are everything.
If I had to say more,
it is forever.

Honey,
your lips.
Your skin,
velvet.
To me,
you are an angel.

You are the meaning
for everything that
ever meant anything.

You are the meaning
of anything that
has a meaning.

YOU are so many things, and all are great.

> You are so sexy,
> as sexy as you can get!
> Surprisingly, everyone else knew
> but you.

What YOU do to me. It's indescribable when I am in your presence, your body, your beauty.

You touch me and turn me on,
and I don't understand.
I can't concentrate.
You have me at your command.

With you,
everything is exciting.
I feel young,
vibrant and alive.
Now I find myself
capable of anything.
Everything is possible.
I can thrive.

You are a damned
distraction.
I hate it,
I love it.
It's so complicated
but I am loving the action.

Your sensuality
and sexuality
excites me.
Your intelligence
and beauty
blinds me.

Your lips excite me.
I love them,
they drive me crazy.
I would love to bite
them very slowly
and never stop
because I adore them.
To me, they are holy.

Your body
is a magnet,
it's sexy hot
and fiery.
You are daily in my diary.

What would I do for YOU? EVERYTHING.

What would I do for love?
For you,
anything,
everything,
anywhere,
anytime.

YOU'RE leaving me? I sincerely hope not because I don't know how I can cope.

My problem is that
I have to share you and
I'm not going to lie,
I would like you to myself,
and you can't understand why.

You are not the first
person I have loved.
I loved you being
the first one
I will always remember.

My gift is to have found you.
My fear is I will lose you.

Some questions for you:

What does he or she do for you? Write it down.

Write ten "YOU are" and share it with them.

If you had to summarise it an a paragraph, thought or poem. What is he or she to you?

What else?

Summarising YOU... It's your humour, your looks, your love, your warmth, your spirit, your inner and outer beauty.

10. BEAUTY

What is beauty? It doesn't only boil down to "looks." No, it's so much more than that. Beauty is everywhere if you look for it. Beauty is in nature, in the simple things, in the thing we take for granted. In a sunrise, in the clouds and sky, observing a river, a mountain, a beach. It's also being kind, caring, loving, compassionate, forgiving, humble, and endearing. These are all beautiful acts. Women and men are beautiful alike. They are all so beautiful in their own unique ways.

Kind, caring and loving people
have one thing in common.
They are all beautiful.

The blind can see beauty for what it is.
Those with vision sometimes miss it.

Anything loving you do is beautiful.

Anything you do lovingly is beautiful.

I try to describe what I envision in my mind. I can't. Words fail me. I cannot find the right words to define your beauty.

Your beauty
is impossible to define.
Maybe divine?

I've been around,
I've seen a few things,
but by far you are
the most beautiful creature
I have ever seen.

Wow, your beauty is divine.
I thank God every day that you are mine.

Her outer beauty is easy to notice.
Her inner beauty is pure bliss.

I've seen beautiful things.
But I've never seen something so beautiful
As you.

What about that heart-melting smile? A smile that melts you,
a smile that leaves you defenceless.

> The beauty of your smile
> opens up my heart.
> It melts me.
> It breaks me.
> I fall apart.
>
> Your beauty makes you powerful,
> your smile makes me powerless.
> It makes everyone powerless.

A beautiful heart. Who doesn't know someone with a beautiful heart that touches everyone?

> The beauty of your heart
> is what sets you apart!
>
> It's your heart,
> It's your soul,
> or is it your beauty.?
> It's like you've given me a potion.
> What I do know is that you are easy to love.
> You are my devotion.

Some people are incapable of seeing how beautiful they are and that itself is beautiful. A few people I love or have loved spring to mind - my daughter, my daughter-in-law, a few ex-girlfriends, and some friends. It surprises me that they regard themselves as average. Sometimes, for example, they might focus on some of the body parts that they tend to dislike, and that might be what makes them so special, what makes them so sexy, and attractive. We are all imperfect in a perfectly beautiful way. Perfection does not exist. We are all made to be as nature intended.

Life is beautiful, you are beautiful.

What's beautiful about you
is that you don't appreciate
your beauty.

So many things make you beautiful.
Not appreciating your beauty is one of them.

Some questions for you

What is beauty to you? Write it down.

Where do you find beauty?

What beautiful things do you take for granted?

What is beautiful about your partner? Share it.

It's so lovely to see and appreciate beauty wherever you find beauty.

But then, in the blink of an eye... things change, especially in a relationship.

It can be all over.

11. FALLING OUT

So, love might be on the way out. It's more difficult to appreciate beauty, to see beauty. Whether amongst lovers, family and friends, love may have a shelf life. Much is said during a relationship, you know...

"I will love you forever, to the moon and back, I adore you..."

... and something happens, a flicked switch, an accumulation of events, a combination of hurtful words. You outgrow each other, you mature, you are enlightened, you change, or want different things. Maybe it's the age difference, cultural barriers, conflicting religious views, or simply the way you both see things or how YOU feel.

> You move on and fall out because
> the mind and the heart
> have stopped speaking.
> One will win,
> one will give.
>
> Just like a cloud disappears from the sky,
> she stopped loving him.
> There was no reason why.
> She moved on.

Ideally, you want to remain kind and civil, but it's easier said than done. You are simply falling apart and falling out.

Just because you have said wonderful things to each other, doesn't mean much. It wasn't forever.

Was it what was said? Or the way it was said?

> Remember, words have meaning
> until they don't.
> Love ends.

What I mean by this is that all love stories end because we are limited by time. If it doesn't end in life, it will end in death.

While you may have agreed once on what love was...

> Love is not what
> you think it is.
>
> Love is not what
> you want it to be.

Maybe the things you found attractive before you might not find attractive anymore. The things you adored, loved, found cute...are not so much anymore.

> I love you.
> Just don't love how complicated you are.
> I love you.
> Just don't love your mood swings.
> I love you.
> Just don't love how you love me.

You start questioning everything.

You made me question love.

You made me question love
when love is unquestionable.

Love is not questionable,
people are.

It's just not there anymore. That "not feeling it" kind of thing and it hurts like a hot stake to the heart. I've been there, I have dished it out and it has been dished to me.

And all you do is question everything.

Was it this, was it that, is it me, is there someone else? What is it, what was it? Which makes me wonder:

> I wonder,
> is it a thought,
> a sentence
> or a situation,
> where suddenly
> love is more of a complication?

When you take your love away,
I suppose you don't feel you have much to say.
When the love is taken,
it doesn't matter how many words they say,
you are convinced they are mistaken.

From afar,
to tell you so often
that I love you
and miss you
hurts.
It hurts too much.
Let's move on.

I am not sure what's worse,
losing the love,
losing the touch, or both.
I don't remember.
I choose not to remember.

But one day... he might fly away.

He was the one who got away.

She fell in love when she didn't want to.
He fell out of love when
she didn't want him to.

Some questions for you:

When falling out, finishing a relationship, have you provided the necessary closure?

What would you have asked your partner to do differently?

What have you learnt? Write it down.

What are the words you should have said, could have said?

What would you like your ex-partner to have done differently or said differently? Write it down. Can you still share it?

It's never too late. Can you still share them now?

Communication, as painful as it may be essential – it's actually vital for closure. It's a minimum gesture to who once was your love. Do it right, keep it tight.

It's happening. This is not going anywhere. I feel so hurt. So distraught. I am lost. I cry every night. I am in a dark place. I can't stop thinking. I can't stop. I can't stop.

What do I feel? Thanks for asking. I feel utterly rejected.

Fasten your seatbelts. We can expect some heavy turbulence.

12. BETRAYAL

Not only have you fallen out, but you have also broken up. It has officially ended, whatever relationship you had. But where did it all go wrong? We will talk about rejection in the next chapter.

Did it end because of betrayal? He or she cheated on you?

If the above is true, it obviously fuels rejection to a much deeper level.

Excuse my brutal honesty again, but I want to open up to my past mistakes.

As you already know, I cheated on my wife several times over the years towards the end of our marriage. I lived a lie, like many conventional marriages, but this is not to excuse myself, let me make that clear. I have had to dig really deep to empathise with what I have done, and how it has caused so much pain to my ex, my kids and our relationship or lack of it. This is not easy to write.

I chose both. I wanted my family and my freedom. Technically, I lived a fake monogamy. I should have left my ex-wife many years earlier. I did what I thought was right. I was wrong.

On your pursuit
to do the right thing,
sometimes you do
the wrong thing.

Betrayal is such a strong word, a heavy word. It's defined as a violation of a person's trust or confidence, of a moral standard...

Those you trust the most
can betray you most.

There are different levels of pain,
but betrayal can actually
make you insane.

You can forgive someone
who betrayed you but you
can never forget.

Once betrayed, can you ever trust?

What hurts most? Is it the lover who betrayed you or the friend? I think it's the betrayal of the friend that hurts most. You start questioning what was real.

How honest should you be? I mean, if you have cheated on your partner, is it better to be completely honest? Come completely clean with everything? Go into details, all the details? I suppose the answer is yes, but are you sure?

Many people who are part of a couple feel they have been cheated on but don't know the details, or do they choose not to know? The "monogamish" factor.

In Spanish, we say, *"ojos que no ve, corazón que no siente,"* meaning, "eyes that don't see, the heart that doesn't feel."

John Lennon said, "being honest will not get you many friends but it will always get you the right ones..." Not sure, John, but I think I agree.

They also say that an open enemy is better than a false friend.

If betrayal comes from cheating, does the "once a cheater, always a cheater" apply? I disagree. Maybe in a new relationship, you should be open from the outset.

Open to express what you want, what you need, your sexual desires. Maybe you choose not to live a lie and be in a relationship where monogamy is not your thing!

I met my ex-wife for lunch when I was finishing this book, and even after four years, she is still hurting. Like on many occasions, she wanted to talk about it. I have apologised many times, but she still can't get past it. It hurts me because I hate to see her hurting, but it also hurts me because I can see the impact this has continued to have on her health.

She can't let it go. And that makes it even worse.

> Seek to forgive
> those that hurt you.
> Choose to live before
> your pain outlives you.
>
> Betrayal brings disappointment.
> Disappointment can make you bitter.
> Bitterness can kill you and your soul.
> Let it go!

A few thoughts on letting go! Let it go.

Let Go

Of what was
Of what never was
Of who you hurt
Of what hurt you
Of what you did
Of what you didn't do
Of what happened
Of what couldn't be
Of who you wanted to be
Of who they wanted you to be
Of what never will be
Of what you can't control
Of those who judge you
Of those who no longer love you
Of those who no longer appreciate you
Of those who don't understand you
Of those who don't want to understand you

I have asked those I hurt for forgiveness. But I seek forgiveness of those I have truly hurt. The rest can Rest in Peace.

> You can apologise
> a thousand times
> and it will never be enough.
> Until you say it's enough.

Some questions for you:

Have you betrayed anyone that you loved? Did you apologise?

What would you have done differently? Write it down.

Can you share it with your ex still?

If you were the cheater, have you forgiven yourself yet?

If not, what are you waiting for?

Let's talk about rejection, shall we?

13. REJECTION

Rejection starts long before it's "official" - non-verbal cues don't lie. You stop holding hands, no kissing - and I mean real kissing - very little eye contact, distance in the bed, no cuddles, maybe no actual sex. You don't have to be a body language expert, you just know. Rejection has started.

One day, I noticed she didn't touch me,
the next I noticed she wouldn't look at me.
I knew. It was over.

She looked at me.
I looked at her.
We knew.
The beginning of the end.

You have a rare way to show
and understand love.
Sometimes you are so loving and
show me affection in a sensual way.
Other times you seem distant and cold.
Your love appears and disappears
just like night and day.

Rejection hurts like hell. For those lucky enough not to remember what it feels like, good for you!

The dictionary defines it as *"the act of not accepting, believing, or considering something."* Well, that sounds pretty harmless and civilised...it is defined in a few cold words, but it's more than that.

Rejection makes you feel what? Like shit? Broken? Hurt? Distraught? Lost? Scared? Alone? It makes you feel numb to the core.

At least that's how I've felt.

> I have a feeling
> that one day
> I won't be feeling
> the numbness
> I feel right now.
> Hope.
>
> You took your love,
> that hurt.
> You took your friendship,
> that broke me.
>
> When you love someone
> as much as I loved you,
> and you still walked away,
> I've learnt, with time,
> and it's easy to say
> there was nothing more
> I could have done
> to make you stay.

Rejection causes PAIN, and so much pain. If I could have wrapped a bandage around my heart, I would have. At times, you feel nothing.

> I'm wanted,
> just not wanted by you.

> I know I am enough,
> just not enough for you.

> If she didn't want you,
> she didn't deserve you.

That's what I say to myself. I don't know if it helps much now but it will help in the future.

> The feeling of not feeling enough
> is enough to make you not feel.
>
> The feeling of not feeling enough
> is enough to make you not feel.
> But remember you are like art.
> It is impossible to be observed
> and appreciated by the blind.
>
> He was smart, but not that smart.
> Not smart enough to let you go,
> or smart enough to see your beauty,
> or smart enough to appreciate your love.
>
> She was smart, but not that smart.
> Not smart enough to let you go,
> or smart enough to see your charm,
> or smart enough to appreciate your love.
>
> There is nothing worse than
> trying to express what you feel
> to someone who doesn't feel.
> Who doesn't feel like you feel.
>
> You got everything,
> except me!

Rejection causes PAIN in capitals, so much pain. If I could have wrapped a bandage around my heart, I would have. At times, you feel nothing.

I feel nothing.
If only I could find
ways to express
how much it hurt,
but it doesn't help.
It's not therapy.
If anything, it's pain.
So, what do I have to gain?
Nothing.

I wonder when it will stop hurting,
but I have this fear
because after weeks, months, and even a year,
it still seems so clear.

She has a way of letting you go,
but he didn't want to go.

Once it's over.
Darkness,
emptiness,
and loneliness
have a whole new meaning.

Rejection makes you lose your mind, and I completely lost mine.

I find it difficult to write
about the moment someone stops loving you.
The reason is because my mind goes blank.
I just don't want to go back.

Sometimes
you have to lose your mind
to get into your head.

Rejection makes you analyse and re-analyse: *was it this, was it that, or was it something else?*

Words have a meaning
until they don't.

Did she or he mean this, did he or she mean that, did she love me? Why did she or he say that?

Out of what you said,
what was meant?
How would I know?

You should have told me
"I love you today"
not forever,
but day by day.
I question
if I will ever trust again?
This not something
I ever wanted to say.

You know what I mean, don't you? Your mind doesn't let up.

All I did was love you.
All I did was love you more.
What part of that were you not sure about?

You would rather be alone
than be with me.
That's food for thought.

Rejection teaches you
simply what we all know,
people are flawed,
and some lie.
Love never does.

Rejection can lead you to a bitter place. In that rollercoaster of emotions, you also get angry!

Up and down, down and up. Fluctuating like the stock market. This place is dark energy. Bad energy.

> You left my life completely
> without a trace.
> I wonder why I deserved
> such coldness and disgrace.
> Was it because I said I loved you?
> I never stopped loving you
> and wanted you back.
> Sorry I was honest,
> and never lied to your face.

Did you get the closure you needed?

I only really understood this once it happened to me. I had not provided closure in the past and that was wrong. Shame on me!

Some people call it Karma.

Perhaps it was not subtle. Perhaps there was NO explanation. I'm off, see ya!

> It's not necessarily
> about letting go,
> but how did she let go?
>
> It's not why did she leave?
> It's how did she leave?
>
> She said, "it's not you, it's me."
> Finally, *something we agreed on.*

And I replied:

> You are less than
> I thought you were.
> So, it's obviously my fault.
>
> She said, "sorry, I'm not feeling it."
> I thought, *"what, your heart?"*

I told her:

"You're not cold, my dear,
you are simply an ice cube
that never melts."

She seems cold.
It's only because
I have felt her love that
I know she's not.

But we can go back to Chapter ONE. Remember to trust love, it has its reasons. You will see it one day. Actions are actions and words are words. Everything happens for a reason, everything is forgivable.

> You shouldn't have taken her
> "I love you's" so seriously.
> Some people say those words
> to anyone or anything.

Not sure if this helps, but something to think about:

> Sometimes,
> the person you loved
> died with that love,
> they are no longer there.

But also think about this, it's important.

> Your ex
> could still
> have deep love for you,
> just doesn't want
> to be with you.
>
> You might take it personal.
> But it's not.

Some questions for you:

If you have felt rejected, what did it make you feel? Write it down.

If you have rejected someone, what would you have done differently?

Is it too late to tell them?

You are broken, you have a broken heart.

14. BROKEN HEART

Rejection is a bitter pill to swallow - it's a tough step to overcome before you begin the process of healing.

To heal, you have to let that broken heart mend back into a whole, gluing it together slowly, letting time do its thing.

In the broken heart phase, you miss that person in your life, and it's quite hard. The phone calls, long talks, video chats, conversations, meals, trips, holidays, favorite places, restaurants, and all those wonderful memories.

You're lost, but it's quite simple, isn't it?

All we want is to be loved.

> All I seek is to be loved.
> Is that too much to ask for?
>
> I've been lost without you.
> Nothing else to add.

But let's start with what having a broken heart represents. To me, it represents pain. Pain is such a complex word, with so much meaning that no more needs to be said, but remember:

We all feel pain differently.

People show pain differently.

Pain from love is temporary.

Your pain cannot be felt by others.

People who don't feel,
don't feel pain.

People who don't feel,
don't feel your pain.

Ex-lovers don't have
to feel your pain.

There is pain that uses you,
and there is pain you use. (Ozark)

Isn't it interesting that the pain in your heart can hurt more than an actual injury to your body? You just wish your heart didn't hurt so much!

My pain is raw,
my heart is sore,
my courage and confidence have gone,
I'm lost now, here and beyond.

Since you went away,
the days seem so long.
All I have is the next morning,
hoping my pain has gone.

I wish my heart
didn't hurt so much.
I wish my pain would just hide.
I just can't keep it all inside.

Trust me,
I don't want to miss you,
I have nothing to gain,
only pain.

For hearts that I have broken.

I broke your heart in so many ways
that words cannot express,
you didn't deserve what I did to you,
I have to say.
All I brought towards the end
of your life were pain and stress.
I hope one day soon
you can forgive me,
and we can move on
because all I have for you is love.
I am grateful,
and I will love you in this life
and far beyond.

You lost your spark,
you lost your smile
along this journey that has been so stressful.
But remember you are very special,
have taken it all on board with so much style,
personally, I will always love you,
never forget and always be grateful.

So, talking about the broken heart, expressing how you feel, and writing it down is a part of the healing process.

> You broke my heart into a million pieces,
> now a million words will attempt to express
> how broken I feel.
>
> Why does it still hurt?
> He asked a friend,
> because it was real.
>
> Why does love
> hurt so, so much?
> He asked.
> It hurts because it mattered.
>
> I smile with difficulty.
> I can't hear the words
> that others speak
> because all I seek
> is you.

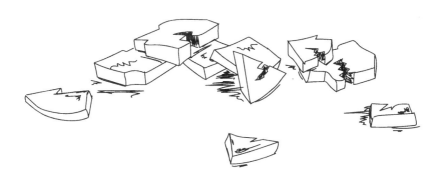

It's a phase of strong, loving feelings, and a broken heart. You know its over, but you still have so much love for your ex.

It's so sad to think
that giving up everything
for you was still not enough.

He wanted to forget her,
but he couldn't.
His love was still so deep.

A thousand lives later,
I will still love you.

Letting you go was hard.
My heart broke
and my head went mad.

When you left my life,
my life left with you.

Ultimate love
is letting go,
I know.
I just can't see it
right now.

I am like a leaf in autumn,
holding onto the tree,
just like your love for me,
it's over, it's clear to see.

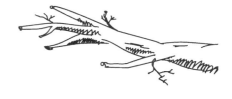

MISSING is a big part. Emptiness moves in and takes over your life. Every room you enter, everything you do... it's without her. Emptiness burns.

> Sometimes, you miss someone so much
> you feel empty.
> But in emptiness, there is space.
> Space for hope.
> Space to learn.
> Space to love.
>
> You left me without leaving.
> I can still remember
> the softness of your lips,
> the warmth of your hand,
> the light in your smile.
>
> It's funny but neither time nor space
> has stopped me wanting to see your face.
>
> I miss you
> like the dry desert
> misses the rain.
>
> I keep travelling
> as far away from you as possible,
> only to keep thinking
> of you wherever I go.

Thinking of you
makes me cry
every day,
not much more
I can say.

It doesn't matter
how hard I try.
I keep missing you,
all I want to do is cry.

And although
I don't see you anymore,
every day I daze,
I wish and pray
those beautiful memories would
always replay
until my final day.

My heart is still close to yours,
putting distance between us
has not helped.

I've travelled far and beyond
and I have realised
that distance
does not make you
any further away from my heart
as I theorised.

I kissed other lips,
and touched other bodies.
But they were not you.

In my mind, I am with you.
In my heart, you never left me.
In my soul, we will be together forever.

Missing you is like thirst,
it always comes back.

What is it you miss?
What is it about her specifically that you miss?
I love this thought, it's:

> The way you held me.
> It's what held me together.

It makes it more difficult.
Broken heart phase "how the hell do I forget you?" HOW?
How can I live without you?
Please, anyone?
Answer... you have to go through it.

It's impossible to forget you
because you are impossible to forget.

How can I breathe
if you are
my air and
my lungs?

My current situation comes
from not knowing how to stop loving you.
It's impossible for me to see a life without you.

You chose you over me,
great for you.
For me…not so much.

Hundreds of songs
remind me of you,
suddenly some music doesn't
sound the same,
some of those words
have a different meaning.

I loved you so
intensely
and for years,
you can't expect me
to stop loving you
immediately,
Overnight.

The deep sadness phase! Oh dear, just get the tissues out, turn the phone off, close the curtains. We are stuck in that kind of phase.

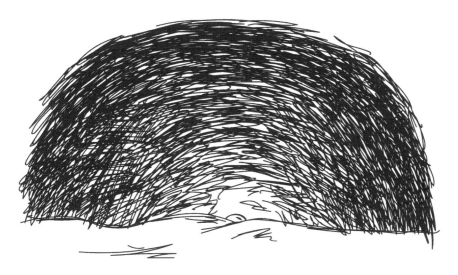

As I walk through
the dark night,
lonely and alone,
I remember vividly my hands
parting yours,
and the space,
time and emptiness
that was left behind.

Darkness is darker,
for me there is no sun
loneliness has expanded,
and my heart weighs a ton.

Life suddenly, "hon,"
is no longer fun.

I was such a fool
to give you my love again
because all you did was cause
me so much pain.

I'm drowning as
if I were at sea,
and although
people are trying to rescue me,
only you can.
I am doomed.

You make me better,
you make me complete,
without you I just see defeat.

I know there's nothing between us,
but it hurts that there is nothing between us.

I've experienced a thousand battles,
and have the scars to prove it.
The biggest scar,
and the biggest battle,
was losing you.

What I feel now,
I won't feel tomorrow.
That's what I hope
because I'm struggling to cope.

You peeled my heart
like an onion,
although it seemed to me
I was the only one crying.

Alone in a cold room,
writing and thinking of you.
When will I come to my senses?

The fool phase.
The phase where you stupidly think "tomorrow she might realise she made a mistake and will want me back." The fool phase
is also called "wake up dude," or "what is wrong with you?"

I know it's supposed to be over,
but can't we live a lie?

What is it I want you to ask?
One last kiss.

What's wrong with me?
With everything
that has happened.
I would do it
all over again.

Your heart is mine,
and although
we are not together,
for me
there will be no other valentine.

It's strange because
I don't want you,
but I need you.
I can't wait to hold
you but I never want
to be near you.
I can't wait
for you to love me again,
yet I don't want your love.

The "I am getting better" phase (very slowly though). The Italians say "piano, piano."

Sometimes, people
won't appreciate your love.
Sometimes, we
don't appreciate the love of others.
God sometimes gives
eyes to those who can't see,
and ears to those who can't hear.

Everything I write about love
and how you make me feel
about you is lost.
I open my heart and don't know why.
I don't know why I do it,
don't know why I even try.

Seeing you again is not a good idea
because I know I will fall in love
with you all over again,
and that is my biggest fear.

You hurt me bad.
Even if I knew what I know now,
I would do it all over again.

.

Can I ever get over this? Will I ever be happy again? Dreaming can become intense.

> The last time I was happy
> I was dreaming of you.
>
> In my dreams I am happy.
> I am with you.
>
> All I dream of is
> dreaming of you.

At times, it seems like you have lost your senses, your character.

The strength I have
comes from the love you gave me.
The weakness I have
comes from you
not loving me anymore.

I sense that it's
senseless to want you,
yet it's all
I yearn for.

I ask myself every day,
will love ever feel the same?

I think I am beyond repair,
but I hope one day
I can look into the stars
and still think of you with love and care.

You hurt me.
I'm lost.
My heart is broken.
I feel exhausted.
My love for you was clean,
Pure, and sweet.
I hope one day you find your match
so he can put you at their feet.

You have to put your
problems and challenges
in context,
and sometimes
the context
is the problem.

I'm not having
a problem with
women wanting me.
The women that want me
aren't the ones I *want* to want me.

Some questions for you:

If your heart has been broken, what did you feel? Write it down.

What would you do differently if it happened again?

What have you learnt? Write it down.

If you broke someone's heart, did you try to empathise with them, I mean *really* empathise?

If so, what did you do?

If you didn't, what would you have done differently?

Broken heart's mend, and life continues. She's gone! He's gone! What's next? Well, it won't be easy!

15. YOUR EXES – AND YOUR FAMILY

Love, family love, can be difficult. I have suffered a lot of family pain and have caused it. I broke up my marriage, I haven't always had a great relationship with my brother, I lost my dad very young, and lost my mum to soon. I had an average relationship with my kids, but I feel that I have let them down.

It's a shame we fall out with the people we should love more and love forever. What is it with family and blood that the connection can be so deeply severed and only death can bring them back to life for you? When my mum died, I had this tremendous emptiness, such a hole in my soul, my heart was so broken, so many regrets about not having spent more time with her.

Mum's love.

If I have one regret,
It's not loving my mother more.
If I was born again, it would be all I lived for.

Arien and bossy,
temperamental and stubborn.
And not an atom in you I would change.
Oh God, how much I loved you.

You were the one I adored.
Wherever you are, I want you to know
that I miss you,
and for me, nothing will be as before.

You gave me so much love, which
I really didn't value,
and all I have is regret.
I love you,
and I adore you.
I am yours,
and you are mine
because for me,
you have not gone,
you're still here,
right by my side.

I regret not speaking,
loving, being even closer
to my mum more often
when she was alive.
Will my kids do the same?
Is that what will revive?

I know because of my mother.
She said: family love,
or lack of love from
a loved one,
hurts like no other.

These are difficult thoughts to share, so personal to me. Although I love my family and appreciate them, I may have let them down or not met their expectations as a father, love should break down any and all barriers.

> If I could go back,
> I would not work so hard,
> so I could create
> more memories.
> Instead, it's left me scarred.

Focus on the love, the loving moments to see what brings you together. Don't allow your memory to be selective.

> Some people,
> especially loved ones,
> have a phenomenal
> ability to forget
> the unforgettable.

Maybe it was you who made the call to pull away. Maybe you just didn't have more to give.

> I gave you everything I had
> for me to be me.
> It seems it still wasn't enough.
>
> I have so much love to give,
> I just couldn't give you more.

But that true and intense love did not disappear. It remains but cannot be felt because it has transformed. It existed, it never goes, it never leaves, we simply choose to ignore it was real because it's safer.

But I think what hurts most is when loved ones choose not to remember, blatantly ignore, or genuinely forget what they took for granted and still they judge you.

I believe the older we get, the less we judge or should judge because we have a better understanding of what life is really all about. We become more empathetic. But remember:

> Some people have a short
> limited memory.
> Or what is called
> a "selective memory"
> where they choose to remember
> what they want,
> never let go and hold tight
> to that grudge.
> You know the ones I mean,
> those that live to judge.
>
>
> Those who judge,
> will be judged.

That's why parents, grandparents, siblings, sons, and daughters must speak, clear the air, forgive and forget, move on, let go.

Unspoken words
are heavy to carry,
they can make you drown.
Unload them before
they destroy you
and bring you down.

I don't know why,
but I'm so good at expressing
what I feel in my mind,
to the air or on the keyboard.
And what I would like
is to say it out loud
to the people I love,
and for whom I would die.

When you lose your lover, part of the pain is losing your best friend, too. What you loved about your lover was that she was warm and caring, she or he was kind and said kind things, she or he complimented, advised and supported you. But when a relationship is over, those mixed emotions can get in the way of remaining friends. That's what makes a break-up harder. I am sure some people do remain friends. When you lose "the friend," it makes it extra hard.

> I've been down,
> in a dark place.
> I needed a friend
> and you were nowhere to be found.
> What happened to
> *"let's be friends forever?"*
> It all becomes clear:
> "Words have no meaning in the end."
>
> You killed me twice in one go,
> first when you left my life,
> second when you took our friendship with you.
>
> You killed me three times in one go,
> first when you left my life,
> second when you took our friendship with you,
> third when I left your heart.
>
> I realise now that we are not friends anymore.
> We were lovers, though.

A girlfriend pointed out that when friendship results from a loving relationship, it's more difficult to remain friends. I tend to disagree but I lack evidence and experience in this dynamic.

Many poets and writers claim that lovers who remain friends either still love each other OR never loved each other to begin with. The truth is, friendships are often broken because the hurt is likely too much and the only remedy is distance. Don't take it personally, send love, and keep the doors wide open.

> I know we are not
> friends anymore,
> but never forget,
> I loved every minute,
> and have no regrets.
> You will always remain
> embedded deep in my core.
>
> If things get tough
> and you feel alone,
> feel you haven't
> got anyone to turn to,
> I'll always be here
> or on the other end
> of the phone.

Based on that principle, are lovers who begin as friends and become lovers more capable of remaining friends?

A story of how much time you have left with....

A friend showed me a campaign for a brand of whiskey which brought friends and families together by surprising them in front of a camera. These people casually talked about their friendships, their favourite moments together, and how they had fun whenever they got together.

The interviewer asked them how frequently they used to meet before, and since then they both had families. It was heart warming, but of course, everyone confessed that they saw each other less and less because "life" complicated things. At one point, the interviewer made them confess exactly how often they saw each other in a year. After this part of the interview, the interviewer went back and forth, leaving the friends and families to chat and asking the group to calculate the total hours they saw each other, converting those hours into the number of days of face-to-face contact.

If they saw each other three or four hours a few times a year, it only equated to an average of five-to-seven days for the remainder of their lives, barring no unforeseen circumstances.

Of course, their faces changed from happiness to sadness as the reality sank in, understanding that if they continued on the same path, they only had a few days left together.

Perhaps this is an important exercise for you. Calculate the hours you have left with your parents, children and friends. You'll be shocked. Unless you do something about it, your time is forever limited. What changes are you willing to make? How can you create more time with loved ones? Think about it! Do something!

Show love to the one you love
when you can love them,
in life.

Enjoy the person who makes you happy.
There within lies happiness.

Don't confuse what's important
with what occupies your time.

You manage your time,
or your time will manage you.

One day will be the last day,
live as much as you can in between.

Some questions for you:

Have you fallen out with any family or loved ones? What can you do to change that? Write it down.

Something you left unsaid to a loved one?

Who do you need to see more often? Write it down.

Who could you see more often? Write it down.

When was the last time you opened yourself up to someone you love?

Can you do it now?

What have you learnt? Write it down.

Are you friends with your ex? Can you go there?

Do you think it's possible to be close friends with your loved one?

Loneliness tends to be your friend, one that comes and goes.

16. LONELY

I have felt very lonely for so many years now, but it has brought me so much quality time. I do feel very alone at times, a situation which has been exacerbated by the Covid-19 pandemic - millions of people around the world have probably felt the same feeling.

It's worse when you are surrounded by people but still feel alone.

> Surrounded by people
> and feeling alone.
> Nothing seems to fill the void.
> I can't ignore it, I feel destroyed.
>
> Hundreds of people around me,
> and I still feel alone.
>
> For so long,
> I feel
> I don't belong
> to anyone,
> anywhere.

Being alone and missing someone you loved next to you.

The worst thing about being alone
is that it means you are not with me.

It's sad to say but
I realise that all I do
is keep checking my phone
because I feel so alone.

I've felt alone for a thousand nights,
And each of those nights,
I thought of you.

Life seems to have less colour, it's grey:

> Life without you
> has very little
> colour and sound.

When you are alone, and you feel sad, deeply sad, maybe cry-ing helps you heal. Nothing wrong with crying. Tears are the way our bodies cleanse, letting go of the pain of what was.

Many times, while I was lonely
alone,
tears filled my eyes.
It cleansed me,
it made me see clearer
it helped me
become wise.

Warriors and heroes also cry.

This brings me to the question, "What is emptiness?" I have felt empty. I still do sometimes. What is emptiness and why do we feel empty, especially when we have so much to be grateful for? Most of us do.

> Complete emptiness
> is an incomplete life.

Is it? Because I have felt that sometimes it can be very fulfilling.

> Being surrounded by emptiness
> can be very fulfilling.

You could be sad, independent of your current relationship situation.

Sadness is the worst of places
where you can't hide who you are.,
You find yourself burrowing down
where you can ignore faces.

I'm alone, and sometimes I'm lonely.
Sometimes, I'm lonely and I'm not alone.

The truth is you come into this world by yourself.
You will leave this world by yourself.

It's in those intense,
lonely moments
when the moments
become intense.

Remember, don't be fooled, the world is full of people who "look" happy but are not. Especially on "social fake media"

> A beautiful smile
> can disguise a
> tremendous unhappiness.

Loneliness, time alone, and pain has helped me boost my creativity. Add some jazz or blues music in the background and anything can happen, only if you try.

Sometimes my loneliness
is full of inspiration.
Sometimes my loneliness
reminds me I feel empty.

When I am alone,
my mind thinks of words to write,
thoughts to think,
ideas to create,
dreams to live,
but I would give it all up
to spend a day with you.

When loneliness steps in,
in those moments of despair,
my creativity seems to flair

Learn to value your time alone. We shouldn't fear being alone. If you think about it, many of us spend very little time on our own from the moment we are born. We are often surrounded by family, siblings, friends, lovers, a wife, a new family, colleagues and associates. You stay married or separate for whatever reason and might want to find someone because you can't stand being alone.

> When being alone is all you have.
> All you have is being alone.
> Shine.
>
> You must learn how to be strong alone.
> Because you alone can be strong.

Learning how to be alone, living alone and choosing to be alone is respectable and understandable.

By choice or preference, I would rather be alone than...

I would rather be alone. And what I mean by that is. . .

(This is an extract from my book, The Question. Find Your True Purpose)

> I would rather be alone if that is what it takes to be true to myself.
>
> I would rather be alone than with people who hurt me or don't believe in me.
>
> I would rather be alone than surrounded by negative people or negative words.
>
> I would rather be alone than with people who don't believe everyone is equal.
>
> I would rather be alone than with someone I don't believe in.
>
> I would rather be alone than with people who don't believe we can make the world a better place.

Remember this: The greatest music, greatest love songs, most inspiring books, most beautiful stories, most amazing inventions, the wildest dreams, and the best comeback stories, have become a reality by people like you and me who were alone, in a room, feeling lonely...

All they had was their thoughts.

> There is greatness
> in your loneliness.

Some questions for you:

Do you spend enough time alone? Why not? Write it down.

Do you enjoy being alone? Why not? Write it down.

What happens when you are alone? Write it down.

What have you learnt from being lonely?

Can your loneliness become the fuel you need to become great?

Even greater than you are?

So, I keep thinking and thinking...let's move on.

17. MOVING ON

Right, so you are back on track, ready to explore, ready to find love, or ready for whatever pleases you. Love continues, love is everywhere.

You got over it, you are moving on with a more positive mindset. You are moving forward. Whatever happened, happened. You have to see that these situations did not happen to you, things happen for you.

On your own you start travelling, meeting other people, becoming more resilient, increasing your resolve and wisdom, and your desire to live your life continues.

Then.

> When you think
> you have lost everything…
> One day, just like that,
> you realise you never did.

Because it's simple.

What was, was.

Part of my sadness was feeling alone, not wanting to be on my own, so I would look for someone. But in part, it is because I don't have a home, a physical home. What is home, anyway? Earlier I said he or she was home. Their arms, their smell, their company.

In these last few years where I have not lived anywhere for more than a few months, I have kept moving, travelling, and that combination of not owning many material items and existing with just a few boxes made me happy, but not having a home made me lonely. I didn't know where I belonged and still don't. I'm working on it.

So, what is home?

> Sometimes, home is someone
> "who is familiar."

But

You are your home.
Home is where your heart and soul lie.

It was there all along,
under my skin.
My heart and soul are my home.
My home is with no one,
or anyone,
and nowhere specific.
It's always been within.

We can forget where home is, but we also seem to suffer
because we also forget...

It is what it is.
Things are as they are.
We suffer because
we imagined different.

You have learnt a few things. You learnt...

Those who disappoint you,
teach you.
Those who hurt you,
make you stronger.
Those who betray you,
make you wiser.

Sometimes you are
not meant to love anyone
apart from yourself.

If you have been misunderstood,
I know you can't see it now,
but trust me, it's all good,
and it all happened for a reason.

Sometimes, after a storm and heavy rain,
you just need to drift,
float in your mind and thoughts
and wait for the next morning.

All of a sudden, you think differently. Something changed in your head, in your mind, in your heart. One day you wake up and it doesn't hurt at all...or not that much.

You can't
hurt me
anymore,
anymore.

I gave you so much love
and so much affection,
but it was all in vain.
That's life sometimes.
It doesn't matter what you do,
you just have to endure the pain.

You stay where you feel loved.
And if unloved is how you feel,
and you can't handle the pain,
away, far and for long you will remain

You are matter,
I am matter.
Love is all that matters.

Sharing my vulnerability has helped me wonders. It was my therapy. Becoming vulnerable, opening up, sharing your feelings, and writing them down. Cathartic.

> From the pieces you left me in,
> the hurt, the hard moments,
> creativity and hope
> have come through just like spring.
>
> Becoming vulnerable
> is hard, very hard,
> but what is the alternative?
> Keeping my feelings inside?
> Not expressing them?
> Becoming cold like you?
> I'll take my chances.

You get over it...

Finding a way to forgive,
is the only way you can live.

Don't hold on
to what let you go.

And once upon a time,
they had enough and moved on.
You can only move on when
you let go.

The only thing that matters is love.

The ultimate proof of love
is letting go.

You can fight.
But sometimes you must let go.

To move on, you have to forgive.
When you forgive, you grow.
When you grow, you become conscious.
When you become conscious, you realise
that love is the only thing worth living for.

Lovers come and go,
but love will remain love.

Remember...let me repeat this.
Remember that...

> People come and leave your life
> to tell us what
> we needed to hear,
> to make us feel what
> we needed to feel,
> to teach us lessons
> we were never taught.
>
> Your darkest,
> scariest challenges
> can also bring the
> brightest,
> bravest moments.

You also believed the "we will be best friends forever story."

Hey, I hope it happens and we can actually be friends, real friends forever... but sometimes they are just good intentions and meaningless words.

I will fight to always be friends with people I have loved deeply. It doesn't make sense not to...

BUT it takes two to tango.

> I thought we would be friends forever
> because when people like you and me
> have loved each other so intensely,
> forever friends we should be.
>
> At the end, promises are just words.

But we need time...time, time, time.

Sometimes it needs
to rain to clear the road.

Slowly I am me again.
Now I am stronger,
unstoppable, and ready
to be me,
but better than then.

Sometimes,
we just need
to let time
do what it does best.

With time, you will realise
that all you needed to do
was to let time do what it does best.

Give time the time.

You are moving on, but you still have moments of anger. It floods back. It's normal, it will simmer for a long time, let me tell you.

> I had this romantic idea that
> we would get back together.
> Romantic? Naive?
> Stupid, really.

> If they don't appreciate
> what you bring.
> Take it elsewhere.

That's why communication with your ex is so important. If you can remain friends, and leave jealousy or hurt aside, you must. Tell your ego to "chill." give it some time out.

Keep talking.

Be there for each other but in the meantime remember:

> Someone out there
> will appreciate your tender touch,
> will feel the warmth
> in your heart,
> the light of your soul
> and the vastness of your love.

But most importantly, hopefully, you will have fond memories of each other to rebuild that friendship and never lose it.

> He didn't want to be with her.
> It was painful,
> but he would continue
> to relive those beautiful moments.

> I've lost big.
> I've lost everything.
> My biggest loss? You.
> Luckily, I still have the memories.

> Those tens of thousands
> of pieces you shattered my heart into
> became words,
> words
> of despair,
> of darkness,
> of hope,
> of love.
> I thank you.

> When you left me,
> I went mad.
> I was numb with pain,
> but it's okay,
> now, once again,
> I feel sane.

Thank you
for the pain
you caused me.
It made me
stronger for longer.

Break-ups are a place
where the soil is rich.
A place from which lessons,
Hope and change
grow.

You hurt me.
I was bitter,
but in the process,
I became stronger,
ready to share
with someone
who would care
and love me
for longer.

Some days are hard.
Some days are great.
Some days you are sad.
Some days you appreciate your fate.

I know there's nothing between us,
but let me dream
since the dream is all I have,
and all I have left.

With everything that happened,
and all the despair,
love for you is all I have,
and all I want to share.

It may sound confusing to you,
but me saying "I love you"
does not mean I want to be with you.
I simply "Love you and always will."

No regrets.
How could I?
If you were
my everything.

It happened because
it was supposed to.
Regret?
Never.
And I will never forget.

Some questions for you:

How difficult was it for you to move on?

How did you do it? Write it down.

What would you do differently?

What have you learnt? Write it down.

What helped you? Write it down

Next? Living...of course. Enjoying this precious life we have been given.

18. LIVE

Enjoy life and what it has to offer. The small things, the things we take for granted, breathing, hearing, breathing, a spring morning, a summer sunset, admiring a tree or forest, a sandy beach, the innocence of your son or daughter. Whatever it is, don't be afraid of making mistakes and falling in love or out of love. Meet new people and learn from people and their actions.

Become wiser, stronger and smarter, but never give up on love.

Be ready to live, smile for no reason, listen to the birds sing and travel. Have fun, enjoy life...

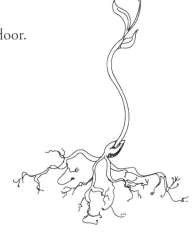

You must be with different people
to learn different things.

You must be open to love
for love to knock on the door.

You must be open to life
to live an open life.

Hope is the seed.
Believing is the water.
Becoming is the sun.

You gave me the winter,
I am waiting for spring,
for the birds to sing.

Not sure why love comes and goes,
but I remain hopeful one day it stays.

Don't despair, my friend,
what is yours is yours,
and will be yours in the end.

Remember you are a human being. But are we "being"? You are a soul having a human experience so don't forget to be.

If the purpose of life is to live,
then make life your purpose.

In being, we live.
And in the process of living,
we forget to be.

The noise of life
distracts us.
And with that distraction
sometimes,
we miss out on life.
Be.

If living is about being.
Be.

Find ways to tap into your consciousness: exercise, meditate, fast and explore into psychedelics.

Protect your body from harm, from what's not good for you. Fuel your mind with ideas and inspiration. Feed your soul with love and loving things.

You have everything you need, everything is within you if you only look. Tap into a higher source, the innate wisdom that has been passed down into your genes from previous generations, and the previous lives your soul has lived.

> One spends a lifetime, and it's sad,
> looking for what you don't have.
> In the end, you realise that
> what you needed, you already had.

> Life can get richer
> not because of
> "things and possessions"
> but because of simplicity
> and lack of them.

Some questions for you:

Are you enjoying life? Are you living? Are you being?

What have you not done yet?

What's on your bucket list? Write it down?

When will you get round to it?

How do you know you have the time to do it?

What are you holding back on?

Looking back at your life till now, what have you learnt so far?

Is TV an important part of your life? Why don't you make your own memories? Get out, live!

The truth is all you need to live your life is, "you." What is meant to be will be, be loving, share love, and spread love, plant the seed and see what happens.

19. THOUGHTS IN MY MIND

If maturity has brought me anything it is for me to become more grateful. In appreciating the simple things in life, but also appreciating the things I have taken for granted for many years:

What do we take for granted? So many things.
Where do you want to start. First of all, physical things:

Our amazing heart that keeps us alive, our lungs and being able to breath, our vision through our eyes, our hearing, our limbs, to be able to walk, to be able to hold and do all sorts of things with our hands, our thinking capacity, our health when we are healthy and the list goes on.

What about the other things like, electric, running water, a roof over our head, food, a vehicle, money to shop for things and the list goes on.

Don't we take so many things for granted? Friends, family, health, love...

The world is not a fair place, humanity focuses on money, on politics, power.

It's time for all of us to start sharing, talking, doing, being kinder and more loving. In finding ways of elevating consciousness, in becoming better humans for our kids and future generations.

> Gratitude,
> simplicity,
> shows your maturity.

I've been through a lot, but far less than many. It's been a balancing act and challenging at times, but also rewarding. Like many of us, I have felt disappointed and let down by people. I have felt fear, been scared and hit rock bottom a few times. On the other hand, I have also disappointed, hurt and let down some people who believed in me. At times, I have been extremely happy, joyful and on top of the world.

Above all, I am very grateful for everything that has happened to me and who I am. Whatever you do, don't give up on living your life, don't let others dictate who you should be.

> In search of that version of you
> that you want to become
> you will lose friends
> and family along the way.
> Because those who know you
> want you to remain the same,
> not to change.
> But be calm,
> don't lose control,
> it doesn't matter.
> For those who truly love you,
> will love your soul.

You pay a high price, to follow your dreams, to have freedom, to not be attached to your partner for so long. I particularly paid the price for my family unit, for our family moments, for feeling part of the family I helped to form.

I'm not the first separated or divorced person to suffer the pain of feeling alone, feeling like a stranger. It is hard to see from a distance how your family and ex-friends get together to spend those beautiful moments together where you are just a mere spectator.

The world is full of separated families, separated by pain, by the inability to forgive, to move on. And it is because of this intransigence that families grow further apart, permanently breaking ties because they are unable to remember what unites them, which is much more than genetics.

> I see my life sometimes as if
> I have not been the main character.
> What was part of me, is no more.
> At times it is sad and devastating.
> But you can't remain pessimistic,
> you have to believe in what you do,
> in who you are,
> create a new life for yourself
> and stay optimistic.

I have learnt a few things about myself:

> I am not so much who I was
> but who I am going to be.
> Because I want to
> become a better man.

As you get older and see your scars,
the pain you have gone through,
the people who have let you down,
and the lonely and dark moments you have had,
you realise that you are stronger
than you thought,
tougher than you ever imagined,
and wiser than you knew.
Suddenly,
nothing scares you,
and no one fazes you.

I've hit rock bottom more times
than I care to remember,
and every time it happened to me,
fear, uncertainty and loneliness
were at the centre.
And then as time passed,
I always learnt a lesson.

The main one is that death
is the only thing that has no solution,
so go on, fight, hold on.
That is the only conclusion.

I've also learnt what I am made of, and what I am capable of.

In hardship I understand
that I am a fighter, a warrior,
that I am brave, with courage,
brave enough not to give up,
to keep on fighting,
and giving my all
as long as there is strength in my hand.

The times I thought
that there was nothing left in me,
I have found strength when there was none,
courage where I had none,
and the ability to fight when I didn't believe.
Resilience.

I have reinvented myself more times
than I can remember.
Provoked by adversity,
necessity.
What's the option?
Surrender?
My future is written,
I believe in myself.
God or the Universe
sends me these challenges
because I am capable and
I have dealt with worse.

At this point in my life, I am going through a massive cycle of creativity, learning and discovery. All I want to do is write, find ways to elevate my consciousness, become a better human, share my views and talk about love. LIFE.

Ego

I realise that a lot of what I wrote was driven by my ego. It was my ego that was hurt and didn't want to let go. I felt betrayed, that someone belonged to me because we had become close. It's that resentment, our anger, and that egotistic mindset that hurts. In the end, we are all souls travelling in body suits given to us at birth.

When in pain again, ask yourself...

What would love do?

Become aware of that pain:

Awareness kills the ego.

> Ram Dass said we suffer because we cling, we cling to things, to relationships, to the pain. It becomes part of who we are, that's why we suffer because we cling. LET GO.

So here I am, finding myself at this ripe old age asking myself more and more questions. I suppose it's better late than never.

I freestyle in saying, "I love you,"
and think that's beautiful.
No apologies.

In that place of vulnerability,
I found myself
and all my deepest thoughts.

The more vulnerable I was,
the more vulnerable I became.
The more vulnerable I felt,
the more I found my true self.

Vulnerability is like an onion.
Keep peeling
each layer and it
will become softer.
Sweeter.

Opening up
and being vulnerable
is hard to do.
What is the alternative?
What are the consequences if you don't?

At times:

I feel like a stranger,
like I'm not part of a pack.
It doesn't matter where I go,
sometimes I question
if I am on the right track.
I feel that my mission
is to write what I feel,
talk about love
and remove the onion peel.
At the moment it seems
that nobody understands me.
But I'll keep trying until the day I die,
because I believe in my message,
although sometimes I would prefer to hide.
I feel it's my calling, but
I think it might be better to keep it bottled inside.

Why is that?

Why do some people feel so comfortable
talking about their bank balance,
or company turnover
but are so fearful
of expressing love,
talking about love
or sharing love?

Why is it so difficult to say "I love you,"
to some people who are close to you,
who mean so much to you?
Especially to those you have loved and cared for dearly.

Why is it so difficult to forgive?
Fear, I think.
Fear of letting go.

At the time of this writing, Will Smith had a public outburst at an Academy Awards ceremony and slapped emcee Chris Rock for saying something Smith felt disrespected his wife. The man had worked his socks off all his life to win an Oscar, and that one brain snap not only punched the lights out of Chris Rock, it also punched the lights out of Will Smith's life and career.

NO man or woman should be judged for what they do in a single moment of lost control. But the fact is we do judge. If we have learnt something from Will Smith, it's that sometimes things can change in the blink of an eye.

Will Smith deserves forgiveness and another chance, as do we all. And remember that when you are on top, things can change and when you are at your rock bottom, without hope, things can change. Having said this, I had friends disputing the fact he should be forgiven. Shame on them! It's not like he is a mass murderer... What would love do?

Remain humble, present, in the now.

> Your best moment
> can become your
> worst moment.
> Your worst moment
> can become
> your best moment.

Me personally...

I'm not going to lie,
I want to love and
be loved by someone
who loves me,
so we can become one.
I want someone who appreciates
me for who I am,
who adores me
until the day I die.

Remember our lives:

Our choices and decisions
either move us away
from love or towards love.
But sometimes, we are at
the mercy of the Universe
and it doesn't matter what you do,
you simply need to surrender.

Be brave... have courage. Never give up.

You must show courage
when everyone is afraid.
You are going to have to smile
when everyone is sad and wants to cry.
You are going to have to lead
when no one else will.
You must step up
when no one else does.
You must love
when everyone else wants to divide or hate.

You are capable of so much more
but you will only discover it
if you are not afraid.
Fear is just a step into the unknown.
And the unknown is the step ahead of
what will make sense afterwards
and will become known.

Don't give up because it's hard,
don't give up because it's unfair,
don't give up because you think you can't.
Surrender is doom
and if in you there is life,
one last breath,
keep going.
Keep going until your death.

The world, life and circumstances
will sometimes seem difficult, unfair,
adverse;
at times, you will feel despair.
But remember that everything
that happens to you
is because you are capable,
capable of so much more,
God, the Universe, knows it.
You just need to realise it.
Don't give up, you are more than able.

In that dark moment,
when you are
trembling,
doubtful and in fear,
that's when you find
the warrior within you.
The one who doesn't give up,
the brave
the hero
will appear.
The end is beautiful.
Fight on

As much as I hate to say it because it sucks:

> Ultimate love
> is also letting go
> of the person
> you love most
> in the world.

And remember, it's your call as to what you focus on:

There are situations and people
from the past
who can drag you down,
or new realities and possibilities
that can pull you around.
You choose which ones
you want to hold on to.

I'm safe now, I am making sure I live by this. I still believe in people and in love, but I won't let my guard down:

> You can't disappoint
> me anymore,
> anymore.

To the women in my life... I thank you.

> If I feel like I do,
> is it thanks to you?
> Thanks for the love,
> thanks for the pain,
> it gave me when I needed
> and what I needed to gain.
> Remembering
> and forgetting
> is how I will remain.

The older I get the more admiration I have for the women who gave me so much, women who have supported me, loved and still love me...

> If I am a better, wiser, stronger, more caring, more sensitive, more vulnerable, more loving man...it's thanks to you.
> Grateful.

Women. Respect to you all. Sending you massive amounts of love and respect. I BELIEVE all women should be in charge of everything, everywhere!

Men being selfish,
believe that women
who give us life
are not entitled
to equal rights.
Believe they are only
good to be daughters or wives.
Shame!

If women give us life,
why do men hide,
deny, forget,
and push them aside?

Simple, really,
we are all only alive
thanks to women.
When did men start
becoming so blind,
so ungrateful,
to not give them
what they need and deserve.

Women
are everything,
life,
love,
work,
consistency,
and intelligence.
They do everything,
and support us,
with extreme elegance.

I think we all know
and can say this
until we are blue in the face.
The world ruled by women
will be a much better place.

Injustice

At the time of finishing this book, Russia (led by President Vladimir Putin) chose to invade Ukraine. Many innocent people suffered, were misplaced, traumatised and died. And the thing is...

There is no debate.
Everything is debatable.

So why do people not talk more? We are all humans with the same needs, destined to end up in the same place, and everything in-between is really not important. The only thing important is love.

Let's look at what brings us together and stop this madness people are getting away with. The world must wake up so unjustified wars like the one in Ukraine and other parts of the world never happen again.

Spread the love!

The world needs YOU, my friend.

The world needs you to:
Love when people hate,
give when people take.
Show courage when people show fear.
Do what needs to be done
Show up, don't disappear.

The world needs you to show up and step up.
Don't hide.

Focus, focus on what you want.

Something to think about:
I know this is a lot.
Don't we tend to focus
on what we don't need to know?
And we don't really know
what we don't know,
although we think we know
what we know.
So why don't we focus on
what we really need to know
before it's too late to ever know?

Listen to the silences. No text messages, no calls, CHECK IN.

Sometimes, it is not what is said.
It's the silences between
conversations you must listen to.

I Hope

My hope is to not lose faith:
In society,
in men,
in women,
in justice,
in love.

One last quote from Alfred Lord Tennyson that a loved one sent me:

"Tis better to have loved and lost than never to have loved at all."

I concur.

My last thought for you:

> You can give up
> on some people,
> but never on love.
> Hope.
>
> You can question everything
> but never question love.
> Love is unquestionable.
>
> Happiness comes from
> appreciating simplicity
> and being grateful.
> There are so many things to be grateful for.

THE END

ABOUT BERNARDO

Bernardo Moya is is the best selling author of The Question, Find Your True Purpose, an international speaker. Founder of The Best You, The Best You EXPO, The Best You Magazine and The Best You TV.

Bernardo is also the creator of The Love Event and has promoted and worked with over a thousand speakers. He has worked with the likes of Dr. Richard Bandler, Paul McKenna, Les Brown, Jack Canfield, Sharon Lechter, Marisa Peer, Greg Reid and many more.

His main focus at this stage of his life is to help people to find ways to become more aware of the important things in life, to find ways to elevate their levels of consciousness, to become kinder, and most importantly to talk about love and share love.

info@thebestyou.co
info@bernardo-moya.com
www.bernardo-moya.com

Working with Bernardo

Bernardo has been an entrepreneur for over thirty-five years and has contributed, partnered, interviewed, and promoted top leaders and experts

His expertise in business, books, coaching, NLP and his brands have helped hundreds of thousands of people to become a better version of themselves.

His brand The Best You, The Best You Magazine, The Best You EXPO, and The Best You TV provides platforms for speakers, coaches, therapists, trainers, and entrepreneurs to connect with a vast audience.

Bernardo Moya

Bernardo Moya

Bernardo Moya

If you are interested in working with Bernardo, to be coached, to be mentored follow this link.

The Question

If you are interested in listening to Bernardo's book The Question. Find Your True Purpose follow this link

A Man Evolving

If you would like to become part of a community, gain access to free resources that are open to discussing love, and sharing love. Follow this link.

More Books From

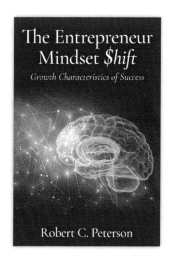

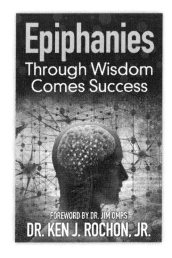

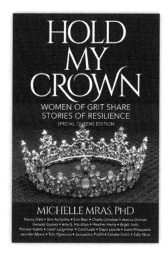

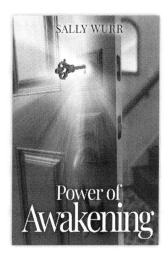

www.PerfectPublishing.com

Made in the USA
Columbia, SC
19 September 2022